Simply Symon Suppers

Clarkson Potter/Publishers
New York

Simply Symon Suppers

Recipes and Menus for Every Week of the Year

Michael Symon
and Douglas Trattner

Photographs by Ed Anderson

Published in the United States by Clarkson Potter/
Publishers, an imprint of Random House, a division of
Penguin Random House LLC, New York.
ClarksonPotter.com
RandomHouseBooks.com

CLARKSON POTTER is a trademark and POTTER with
colophon is a registered trademark of Penguin Random
House LLC.

Library of Congress Cataloging-in-Publication Data has
been applied for.

ISBN 978-0-593-57968-8
Ebook ISBN 978-0-593-57969-5

Printed in China

Photographer: Ed Anderson
Recipe Developer: Katie Pickens
Food Stylist: Susan Spungen
Prop Stylist: Maeve Sheridan
Editor: Raquel Pelzel
Editorial Assistant: Bianca Cruz
Designer: Robert Diaz
Production Editor: Joyce Wong
Production Manager: Philip Leung
Compositor: Merri Ann Morrell
Copy Editor: Kate Slate
Indexer: Elizabeth Parson
Marketer: Stephanie Davis
Publicist: Erica Gelbard

Book and cover design by Robert Diaz
Cover photographs by Ed Anderson

10 9 8 7 6 5 4 3 2 1

First Edition

This cookbook is dedicated to Emmy and Butchie, my precious grandchildren. I love you both more than words can say.

Contents

Holidays

Desserts

Batch Cocktails

Introduction

Hello everyone! I hope you all are as excited about this book as I am. This is my eighth cookbook, and it is one that I've wanted to write for a long time because it is so personal. The recipes in this cookbook really reflect the way we ate as a family and the way Liz and I enjoy cooking and entertaining these days.

As a kid growing up in the Midwest, we ate dinner together as a family every single night of the week. We sat around the kitchen table and talked about our days, our upcoming plans, and what needed to be done around the house. At that table, over those meals, we laughed, cried, and yelled (and when you have a Mediterranean mother, that can all happen at the exact same time!). The high point of every week was the big Sunday Supper, which was either prepared at our house or at my grandparents'. Those festive, joyous, indulgent meals were such a meaningful tradition for me as a child that I continue to host them for my family and friends to this day. Given everybody's hectic schedules, we might not be able to gather every Sunday, but we do eat together as a family as much as possible, and we almost always try to carve out the time for a Sunday supper—even if it happens on a Monday (or holiday!) instead. The recipes in this book come straight from those memorable, occasionally emotional weeknight dinners, those celebratory Sunday feasts, and the meals that I make at home for loved ones today.

Sticky Pork Ribs,
page 89

The first four chapters in the book focus on time of year—because let's face it, while I may crave a hearty bowl of beef stew on a chilly, crisp day, I crave steak off the grill when it's hot outside and the grill is lit. Growing up in Cleveland, I really enjoyed experiencing separate and distinct seasons. Moving from the cool, breezy days of autumn into the bracing chill of winter, and finally the promise and warmth of spring provided a natural rhythm to life, while always giving you something to look forward to. As a chef, cooking this way just makes perfect sense. You get to enjoy ingredients at their absolute peaks, while being able to look forward to what's coming next at the markets. Personally, I think having a food readily available every single day of the year makes it a little less special. In-season foods are often less expensive and, if you shop at local farmers' markets like I do, more sustainable for the planet as they are not shipped on a plane halfway across the globe.

Within each seasonal chapter, I grouped the recipes into complete meals, typically with mains, sides, salads, and sauces. This is how I plan, shop, and prepare meals at home, so that format just feels natural to me. I included tips, when appropriate, to help you plan out your approach and make your cooking as efficient as possible. That said, feel free to mix and match anything and everything in this book to your heart's content! Cooking and eating should be enjoyable, so do as you and your family and your guests please. For those of you that have been Fixing It with Food from my previous two cookbooks (*Fix It with Food* and *Fix It with Food: Every Meal Easy*), on page 334 you'll find an index where we have identified whether each recipe in the book is flour-free, dairy-free, or meat-free. We want to make it as clear and easy as possible for everyone to continue avoiding those triggers so you can eat and feel your best, while still cooking and eating delicious food.

When it comes to holidays, I have to admit that I'm a giant kid at heart. I do love a good party and I tend to go a little (okay, a lot!) overboard when it comes to preparing big holiday meals. Don't worry, I didn't go too, *too* crazy when coming up with the holiday meals for this book. I think they strike the perfect balance between festive and feasible. To make planning for those large family gatherings a little easier, because I know it can be stressful, I've included "Symon Says" boxes. These useful guides will help you map out the whole meal planning process to hopefully alleviate some pressure so that you can enjoy being with your family and friends.

As many of you know, I love dessert! But the truth is, I don't always enjoy preparing them. So the recipes in the chapter on desserts come not just from me, but also Lizzie and my culinary director and friend Katie Pickens (who has tested every recipe for every cookbook and TV show we have ever done). For each dessert, we strive to achieve maximum flavor and enjoyment while keeping the recipes as manageable and straightforward as possible. I think you'll agree when you start making them (they're so easy, even I can make them!).

And last but definitely not least are the cocktails! For this book, I included a selection of my favorite adult sippers, but I converted individual servings into batch recipes. Batching cocktails is just a fancy way of saying "a large quantity of a single beverage made in advance!" This way, when those first guests show up at your door, you don't have to drop everything and whip up a drink. Simply fill a glass with ice, grab that pitcher of Kentucky Mules or Campari Spritzes, garnish, and get the party started!

I have to stop and pinch myself sometimes when I think about the fact that this is my eighth cookbook. Without the love and support of fans like you, who truly inspire and encourage me to write these books, I would not have made it this far. I love every single book that I have written, but if I'm being honest here, this one might be my new favorite. Coming up with the recipes was a labor of love that conjured so many amazing memories of growing up, but also the new memories that I'm creating as a grandfather myself. I hope that some of these recipes become a small part of your family traditions as well.

So please enjoy, have fun cooking, and Live to Cook!

- -

A note about salt: In my kitchen, I cook exclusively with Diamond Crystal kosher salt. It has a completely different texture from brands like Morton, making it less salty per pinch. A good rule of thumb is to reduce the volume by half when substituting Morton for Diamond Crystal.

Frozen Old Fashioned,
page 319

Sunny Days, Cool Nights

Spring is a magical period of transition. In the Midwest, as with many parts of the country, the weather often ping-pongs from winter to summer and back again, sometimes in a single day! As much as you'd like it to be warm, clear, and calm outdoors, Mother Nature has a not-so-subtle way of reminding you what month it is. But little by little, the cold begins to subside, the mornings get a few degrees warmer, and long-dormant plants begin to emerge from the earth. Soon, markets fill up with seasonal produce like lettuces, asparagus, radishes, ramps, spring onions, English peas, and strawberries.

This is also a period of transition in the kitchen. While the urge to stay warm and well-fed with heavier dishes lingers, I'm often inspired to lighten things up by swapping the roasted squashes and pureed root veggies of winter with light, crisp, and raw vegetable-based salads. To me, there is nothing better than that first Shaved Asparagus Salad (page 31) of the season. Other sides, like the Herby Couscous (page 28) and Olive and Orange Relish (page 28) that go with the Braised Lamb

Shanks (page 26), take advantage of the tail-end of citrus season.

As with all the following chapters, these recipe pairings should be looked at as suggestions, not rules. Just because I like to serve the Chicken Cacciatore (page 48) with Pea Greens Caesar (page 50) doesn't mean that it wouldn't be just as delicious accompanied by the Grilled Asparagus and Lemon (page 61). The same goes for the ingredients within each dish. If you happen to spy some ramps at a farmers' market, try substituting them for onions or garlic in a recipe. If you find some morels at a decent price, go ahead and use them in place of portobellos. The only important thing is to be creative and have fun.

Manicotti Stuffed with R
and Spinach, pa

CLASSIC PAELLA + CITRUS SALAD

Serves 4

Despite being a huge fan of paella for as long as I can remember, it was only in the past decade or so that I began cooking it myself. This colorful, celebratory dish is ideal for entertaining because it goes straight from the stovetop (or grill!) to the table in the same pan. It's also great for crowds of any size because it's easy to scale up or down and it's endlessly flexible when it comes to the main ingredients. This recipe pairs juicy chicken thighs with sweet and briny clams and shrimp. The pop of acidity from the Citrus Salad (page 22), cuts through the depth and richness of the paella, and is the perfect accompaniment.

2 medium white onions, chopped (about 1½ cups)
1 medium red bell pepper, chopped (about 1 cup)
1 small jalapeño, seeded and chopped
5 medium garlic cloves, sliced
4 bone-in, skin-on chicken thighs
Kosher salt and freshly ground black pepper
1 tablespoon extra-virgin olive oil
1 teaspoon sweet paprika

1 teaspoon ground cumin
1 cup short-grain rice, such as Calasparra or bomba
1 cup dry white wine
1 teaspoon saffron threads
4 cups chicken stock
12 littleneck clams, scrubbed
12 large shell-on shrimp, deveined
½ cup fresh flat-leaf parsley, leaves and tender stems
Citrus Salad (page 22)

1. In a blender or food processor, combine the onions, bell pepper, jalapeño, and garlic and pulse to a coarse puree.

2. Season both sides of the chicken with a few pinches of salt and twists of pepper.

3. Set a large pan or skillet over medium heat. Add the olive oil and heat to shimmering, then add the chicken skin-side down. Cook, without flipping, until golden brown and crisp, about 5 minutes. Using a spatula or tongs, flip and continue cooking for 5 minutes. Transfer the chicken to a plate.

4. To the same pan, add the vegetable puree along with a pinch of salt. Cook, stirring occasionally, until the vegetables soften and begin to brown, about 5 minutes. Add the paprika, cumin, and rice and cook, stirring occasionally, until fragrant, about 30 seconds. Add the white wine and deglaze the pan, scraping with a wooden spoon to loosen the browned bits on the bottom. Add the saffron and chicken stock and stir to combine. Return the chicken to the pan, nestling the pieces skin-side up in the rice. When the liquid in the pan returns to a simmer, neatly arrange the clams and shrimp between and around the chicken pieces. Cover and cook until the clams open and the rice is tender throughout and crisp on the bottom, about 15 minutes.

5. Garnish with parsley. Serve with the citrus salad.

(recipe continues)

Citrus Salad

Serves 4

3 navel oranges
2 celery stalks, very thinly sliced
  (about 1 cup)
½ cup whole celery leaves
½ cup fresh cilantro leaves
1 small red onion, thinly sliced
  (about ½ cup)

Kosher salt and freshly ground
  black pepper
1 teaspoon ground coriander
1 tablespoon sherry vinegar
3 tablespoons extra-virgin olive
  oil, plus more for drizzling

1. With a sharp knife, slice the ends off the oranges. Then, setting the fruit on one of the cut ends, follow the shape of the fruit to cut off the peel, pith, and membrane (try to remove as little of the fruit as possible). Slice the fruit crosswise into ¼-inch-thick wheels (use the tip of a paring knife to remove any seeds).

2. In a medium bowl, combine the sliced celery, celery leaves, cilantro, and onion and toss to combine. Season with a few pinches of salt and twists of black pepper. Add the coriander, vinegar, and olive oil and toss to evenly coat.

3. Arrange the orange slices on a platter, mound the celery mixture on top, drizzle with some more olive oil, and season with more black pepper.

Pita Bread, page 31

BRAISED LAMB SHANKS
+
HERBY COUSCOUS
+
OLIVE AND ORANGE RELISH

Serves 4

In Greek homes, Easter is not Easter without lamb, typically whole spring lambs spit-roasted over an open fire, but also bone-in leg roasts cooked in the oven. Here's another route you can take. Lamb shanks not only are more manageable to work with and less expensive than leg roasts (and whole lambs, obviously), but they have an incredibly rich flavor, too. When they are slowly braised in liquid, they become meltingly tender as well. Here, the braising liquid is enriched with rosemary, olives, lemon zest, and anchovies, which make everything taste a little better. If you don't have a tin of anchovies on hand but do happen to have a bottle of fish sauce, you can swap ½ teaspoon for the anchovy. I like to serve the lamb on a bed of fluffy herb-flecked couscous to absorb the lamb's amazing juices and then top it all with an orange and olive relish loaded with mint—because nothing goes better with lamb than mint!

1 cup all-purpose flour
Kosher salt and freshly ground
    black pepper
4 lamb shanks (about 1¼ pounds
    each)
5 tablespoons extra-virgin
    olive oil
2 large yellow onions, thinly
    sliced (about 2 cups)
3 medium garlic cloves, sliced

1 anchovy, chopped, or a splash
    of fish sauce
1½ cups dry white wine
Grated zest of 2 lemons
    (about 1 tablespoon)
3 sprigs fresh rosemary
½ cup pitted Cerignola olives
1½ cups chicken stock
Herby Couscous (page 28)
Olive and Orange Relish
    (page 28)

1. Preheat the oven to 300°F.

2. Place the flour in a large bowl and season with salt and pepper. Season the lamb on all sides with salt and pepper. Dredge the lamb in the seasoned flour, making sure to coat all sides well. Shake off the excess.

3. Set a large heavy-bottomed pot or Dutch oven over medium-high heat. Add 3 tablespoons of the olive oil and heat to shimmering, then add the lamb. Cook until golden brown on all sides, about 15 minutes. Use a slotted spoon to transfer to a roasting pan when done.

4. Drain and discard the fat in the pot. Wipe out the pot and set it over medium heat. Add the remaining 2 tablespoons olive oil and heat to shimmering, then add the onions, garlic, and a pinch of salt. Cook, stirring occasionally, until the vegetables soften, about 3 minutes. Add the anchovy and cook, stirring, until aromatic, about 2 minutes. Add the wine, bring to a gentle boil, and cook until the liquid has reduced by one-third, about 5 minutes. Add the lemon zest, rosemary, olives, and chicken stock. Return the mixture to a simmer.

5. Carefully pour the sauce over the lamb shanks in the roasting pan, cover the pan tightly with foil, and braise in the oven for 2 hours.

6. Remove the pan from the oven, remove the foil, use tongs to flip the lamb shanks, and check the level of liquid in the pan. If it is lower than two-thirds the way up the shanks, add water to reach that level. Re-cover the pan tightly with foil, return to the oven, and cook until the lamb is fork-tender, about 50 minutes.

7. Serve with the herby couscous and olive and orange relish.

Symon Says

The lamb shanks can be braised and refrigerated in their braising liquid for up to 2 days. Cover the lamb with foil and warm them in a 300°F oven for 30 to 45 minutes before serving.

The orange relish can be refrigerated for up to 2 days. Allow it to come to room temperature before serving.

(recipe continues)

Herby Couscous

Serves 4

1 cup chicken stock
3 tablespoons extra-virgin
  olive oil
Kosher salt and freshly ground
  black pepper

1 cup couscous
1 cup finely chopped fresh
  flat-leaf parsley
½ cup thinly sliced fresh mint

1. In a large saucepan, combine the chicken stock and 1 tablespoon of the olive oil and bring to a gentle boil over medium-high heat. Season with a pinch of salt and twist of pepper. Add the couscous, stir, cover, remove from the heat, and let stand for 5 minutes.

2. Remove the lid, fluff the couscous with a fork, and stir in the parsley, mint, and remaining 2 tablespoons olive oil. Taste and adjust for seasoning, adding salt and pepper as needed.

Olive and Orange Relish

Serves 4

2 navel oranges
1 cup sherry vinegar
1 cup sugar
1 garlic clove, thinly sliced

1 small yellow onion, finely
  chopped (about ½ cup)
1 cup oil-cured Moroccan olives,
  pitted
½ cup finely chopped fresh mint

1. With a vegetable peeler, remove 5 large strips of zests from each orange, for a total of 10. Roughly chop and set aside.

2. With a sharp knife, slice the ends off the oranges. Then, setting the fruit on one of the cut ends, follow the shape of the fruit to cut off the peel, pith, and membrane. Cut the fruit into small cubes (remove any seeds as you go) and set aside along with any accumulated juices.

3. In a medium saucepan, combine the vinegar and sugar and bring to a simmer over medium heat, stirring to dissolve the sugar. Add the oranges (and any juices), orange zest, garlic, and onion. Return the mixture to a simmer and cook, stirring occasionally, until the mixture reduces and thickens to a jam-like consistency, about 40 minutes.

4. Allow to cool slightly before stirring in the olives and mint.

HUMMUS WITH SPICED BEEF AND PINE NUTS
+
SHAVED ASPARAGUS SALAD
+
PITA BREAD

Serves 4

(with leftover hummus for snacking)

If you have any of my previous cookbooks, you've probably come across a few recipes for hummus. That's because I love hummus and think it goes great with so many foods, from crunchy raw veggies to savory falafel. But another reason it keeps popping up is because Katie Pickens, my longtime culinary director, a brilliant chef, and friend, is absolutely obsessed with chasing down the perfect recipe. Well, she's somehow managed to improve upon her technique to land on what I think is the world's best hummus recipe—her secret? Ice water! This hummus is nutty, smooth, and creamy—a perfect backdrop for earthy beef and pine nuts. To serve, I like to make a little well in the middle of the hummus with the back of a spoon and ladle the beef and pine nuts into the center. It makes for a beautiful presentation. In the spring, I prefer raw, shaved asparagus over cooked, and this salad cannot be any simpler to put together. Of course you need something to scoop it all up, and nothing is as good as warm, puffy, freshly baked pita. Sure, you can use store-bought, but I think you'll enjoy the process of making your own and find the results are more than worth the effort.

Hummus

4 (15-ounce) cans chickpeas, drained (reserving ¼ cup of the liquid and chilling it; discard the rest)
12 medium garlic cloves, unpeeled
½ cup fresh lemon juice, plus more to taste
2½ teaspoons kosher salt
1⅓ cups tahini
1½ cups ice water

Spiced Beef

1 tablespoon extra-virgin olive oil
1 pound ground beef (80% lean)
Kosher salt and freshly ground black pepper

½ cup pine nuts
2 medium yellow onions, finely chopped (about 1½ cups)
3 medium garlic cloves, minced
½ teaspoon ground cinnamon
1 teaspoon Aleppo pepper
1 teaspoon sweet paprika
2½ teaspoons ground cumin
½ cup beef or chicken stock
⅓ cup thinly sliced flat-leaf parsley

For Serving

Extra-virgin olive oil
Shaved Asparagus Salad (page 31)
Pita Bread (page 31)

1. Make the hummus: In a medium saucepan, combine the chickpeas with enough cold water to cover by a few inches. Bring to a boil over high heat, reduce the heat to medium to maintain a strong simmer, and cook until the chickpeas are completely soft and falling apart, about 1 hour.

2. Meanwhile, in a blender, combine the garlic (papery skins included), lemon juice, and salt and process to a pulpy puree. Transfer to a bowl and let sit for 5 minutes to allow the garlic to mellow. Strain through a fine-mesh sieve set over a medium bowl, discarding any solids. Whisk in the tahini until very thick and well combined. Whisking constantly, slowly add the ice water to produce a smooth sauce.

(recipe continues)

3. While still warm, drain the chickpeas (discarding the cooking liquid) and add them to a blender along with the tahini mixture. Process until smooth, about 3 minutes. Add the chilled reserved chickpea liquid from the can and process until very smooth and whipped, about 3 minutes. Taste and adjust for seasoning, adding more lemon juice as desired.

4. Make the spiced beef: Set a large skillet over high heat. Add the olive oil and heat to shimmering, then add the ground beef. Cook, stirring with a wooden spoon to break up the meat, until well browned, about 5 minutes. Season with a pinch of salt and twist of black pepper.

5. Add the pine nuts, reduce the heat to medium, and cook until the pine nuts are toasted and fragrant, about 1 minute. Add the onions and garlic, season with salt and black pepper, and cook until the vegetables soften and begin to brown, about 5 minutes.

6. Add the cinnamon, Aleppo, paprika, and cumin and cook, stirring, for 30 seconds. Add the beef stock and deglaze the pan, scraping with a wooden spoon to loosen the browned bits on the bottom of the pan. Remove from the heat and stir in the parsley.

7. To serve, add about 1 cup hummus to each plate (refrigerate the rest of the hummus for up to 1 week). Use the back of a spoon to make a well in the center and divide the spiced beef among each serving. Drizzle with olive oil and serve with the shaved asparagus salad and pita bread.

Symon Says

The hummus can be made up to 3 days ahead of time. Let it sit out at room temperature for 30 minutes before serving to let the chill come off of it.

Shaved Asparagus Salad

Serves 4

1 large bunch thick green
  asparagus
4 scallions, white and light-green
  parts only, thinly sliced

Kosher salt and freshly ground
  black pepper
2 tablespoons extra-virgin
  olive oil
Juice of 1 lemon

Use a vegetable peeler to shave the asparagus into long, thin ribbons. Transfer to a bowl, add the scallions, and season to taste with salt and pepper. Add the olive oil and lemon juice and gently toss to combine.

Pita Bread

Makes eight 8-inch pitas

1⅓ cups lukewarm water
  (about 110°F)
¾ teaspoon active dry yeast
1 tablespoon honey

3¾ cups bread flour, plus more
  for rolling
2 teaspoons kosher salt
1½ tablespoons olive oil, plus
  more for misting

1. In a stand mixer fitted with the dough hook, combine the water, yeast, and honey and let sit until very foamy, about 10 minutes. Add the flour, salt, and olive oil and blend on low until the dough comes together into a mass, about 3 minutes.

2. Portion the dough into 8 equal balls. Place the balls on a sheet pan, mist them with olive oil, cover tightly with plastic wrap, and refrigerate overnight.

3. Remove the dough from the refrigerator 1 hour before baking.

4. Preheat the oven to 475°F. Place a baking steel or cast-iron griddle (or other large, shallow cast-iron pan) on the bottom rack to preheat. Place a small pan of water on the floor of the oven.

5. Turn the dough out onto a lightly floured surface and roll each ball out to an 8-inch round. Let stand for 10 minutes. Working with one round at a time (or more if space on the steel or griddle allows), carefully transfer a dough round to the preheated steel or griddle and cook for 1 minute. Flip and cook for another minute, then remove to a sheet pan. Repeat with the remaining dough rounds.

6. Serve immediately or store for up to 3 days in an airtight container.

PAN-ROASTED PORK CHOPS AND ONION GRAVY
+ SHAVED SPRING ONION SALAD

Serves 4

Growing up, there were few meals that I looked forward to more than pork chops and applesauce. (So Midwestern of me, I know.) As wonderful as those chops were, this recipe kicks them up more than a few notches. I dust the pork chops in flour seasoned with paprika, salt, and pepper, pan-sear them, and then smother them in a rich and thyme-y onion gravy inspired by Lizzie's mom, who has Southern roots. I like to serve the arugula, spring onion, and fennel salad right on top, but feel free to keep it on the side if you prefer.

½ cup plus 3 tablespoons all-purpose flour
½ teaspoon sweet paprika
4 thin-sliced boneless pork chops, about ¼ inch thick
Kosher salt and freshly ground black pepper
1 tablespoon extra-virgin olive oil
Small bunch of fresh thyme
1 small fresh bay leaf

2 tablespoons unsalted butter
1 cup peeled cipollini onions
2 cups whole milk
½ teaspoon freshly grated nutmeg
¼ cup finely chopped fresh flat-leaf parsley
Shaved Spring Onion Salad (page 34)

1. In a shallow bowl, blend together ½ cup of the flour and the paprika. Season both sides of the pork with a few pinches of salt and twists of pepper. Working with one piece of meat at a time, dredge the pork in the flour, making sure to coat both sides well. Shake off the excess.

2. Set a large skillet over medium-high heat. Add the olive oil and heat to shimmering, then add the pork chops. Cook, without moving, until golden brown, about 5 minutes. Flip the chops, reduce the heat to medium, and cook until golden brown on the second side, about 5 minutes. Transfer the cooked pork chops to a plate and tent with foil while you make the gravy.

3. Drain any oil from the skillet and wipe it clean. Bundle up the thyme and bay leaf in butcher's twine and set the herb bundle aside.

4. Set the skillet over medium heat. Add the butter and heat until melted, then add the onions. Season with a pinch of salt and twist of pepper. Cook until the onions are golden brown, about 3 minutes per side. Add the remaining 3 tablespoons flour and cook, stirring, for 1 minute. Whisking constantly, slowly add the milk. Bring to a boil, then reduce the heat to medium-low to maintain a gentle simmer. Add the herb bundle and nutmeg, season liberally with salt and pepper, and cook, stirring occasionally, for 15 minutes. Remove the herb bundle and stir in the parsley.

5. Top the pork chops with onion gravy and serve with the spring onion salad.

(recipe continues)

Shaved Spring Onion Salad

Serves 4

3 tablespoons white wine vinegar
1 teaspoon Dijon mustard
⅓ cup extra-virgin olive oil
4 cups arugula or any soft green
1 small bunch spring onions,
  thinly sliced (about 1 cup)

1 medium fennel bulb, thinly
  sliced (about 1 cup)
Kosher salt and freshly ground
  black pepper

In a large bowl, whisk together the vinegar, mustard, and olive oil. Add the arugula, spring onions, and fennel. Season with a pinch of salt and twist of pepper and toss to combine.

Sunny Days, Cool Nights

VEGGIE MOUSSAKA + HERBY BRAISED GIGANTE BEANS

Serves 6 to 8

Although my yiayia probably never made a vegetarian moussaka, I'd argue that this version is every bit as delicious and comforting as one made with ground beef or lamb. This hearty casserole features layers of tender potatoes, roasted eggplant, a flavorful tomato sauce, and a creamy, cheesy béchamel. While baking, it fills the house with the most amazing aroma, only to exit the oven all golden brown, bubbling, and beautiful. Although there are more than a few steps in this recipe, each is pretty straightforward and uncomplicated. If you can't chase down gigante beans, go ahead and substitute dried or canned limas. I know lima beans don't have the most glamorous reputation, but when finished in a rich sauce seasoned with tomatoes, honey, and a touch of fresh dill, they are truly amazing. If you have leftover beans, add a little water or stock to the pan when reheating them to loosen them up again.

2 large eggplants, peeled and cut into ½-inch-thick rounds
Kosher salt
2 tablespoons extra-virgin olive oil
Freshly ground black pepper
1 tablespoon dried oregano
3 russet or sweet potatoes, peeled and cut into ½-inch-thick slices

Ragout

1 tablespoon extra-virgin olive oil
2 medium garlic cloves, minced
2 large yellow onions, finely chopped (about 2 cups)
Kosher salt
1 tablespoon finely chopped fresh rosemary
1 teaspoon dried oregano
2 cups dry red wine
2 (15-ounce) cans whole peeled tomatoes, undrained

2 (15-ounce) cans chickpeas, drained and rinsed
¼ teaspoon ground cinnamon
1 bay leaf
Freshly ground black pepper

Béchamel

6 tablespoons unsalted butter
½ cup all-purpose flour
2½ cups whole milk
1 teaspoon freshly grated nutmeg
1 teaspoon kosher salt
Freshly ground black pepper
1 cup grated Pecorino Romano cheese
2 large egg yolks
Grated zest of 1 lemon

Assembly and Serving

¾ cup crumbled Greek feta cheese
Extra-virgin olive oil, for drizzling
Herby Braised Gigante Beans (page 39)

1. Preheat the oven to 375°F.

2. Arrange the eggplant slices in a single layer on a sheet pan. Season both sides of the eggplant with salt and set aside for 15 minutes to pull out excess moisture. Using paper towels, pat the eggplant slices dry. Drizzle both sides of the eggplant with the olive oil, season both sides with black pepper and sprinkle on the oregano. Transfer to the oven and bake for 15 minutes. Flip the eggplant and continue baking until the eggplant is soft and beginning to brown, about 10 minutes.

(recipe continues)

3. Meanwhile, add 1 tablespoon kosher salt to a medium pot of water and bring to a boil over high heat. Add the potatoes and cook until just tender, about 8 minutes. Drain and set aside.

4. Make the ragout: Set a large saucepan over medium heat. Add the olive oil and heat to shimmering, then add the garlic, onions, and a pinch of salt. Cook, stirring occasionally, until the vegetables soften, about 8 minutes. Add the rosemary, oregano, and wine and cook for 5 minutes. Add the tomatoes and their liquid, crushing the tomatoes with your hands as you add them. Add the chickpeas, cinnamon, and bay leaf. Bring to a boil, then reduce the heat to medium-low to maintain a gentle simmer. Cook, stirring occasionally, until reduced and slightly thickened, about 35 minutes. Remove and discard the bay leaf. Season with a pinch of salt and twist of pepper.

5. Make the béchamel: Set a large saucepan over medium heat. Add the butter and allow to melt, then add the flour and cook, while whisking, for 1 minute. Whisking constantly, slowly add the milk. Bring the sauce to a boil, then reduce the heat to medium-low to maintain a gentle simmer. Add the nutmeg, salt, and a few twists of black pepper. Cook, stirring frequently, for 20 minutes. Remove from the heat, add the pecorino, and whisk until the cheese has melted. Set aside to cool slightly, then add the egg yolks and lemon zest and whisk to blend.

6. Assemble the moussaka: Arrange the potatoes in a single layer over the bottom of a 9 × 13-inch baking dish. Add half the ragout and smooth it out to an even layer with a spatula. Arrange the eggplant slices on top, overlapping slightly if necessary. Add the remaining ragout and smooth it out to an even layer.

7. Pour the béchamel onto the casserole and smooth it out to an even layer. Sprinkle with the feta and drizzle with olive oil.

8. Transfer to the oven and bake, uncovered, until golden brown and puffy, about 40 minutes. Let stand for 10 minutes before slicing.

9. Serve the moussaka with the gigante beans alongside.

Symon Says

You can make and then chill the ragout and béchamel for the moussaka up to 2 days ahead of time.

Gently reheat both over medium-low to warm through before assembling your moussaka.

The beans can be refrigerated up to 2 days before serving. Save some of the bean cooking liquid to loosen up the beans when they are being reheated.

Herby Braised Gigante Beans

Serves 4 to 6

2 cups dried Greek gigante beans or giant lima beans
2 tablespoons extra-virgin olive oil
2 small red onions, diced (about 1 cup)
2 medium carrots, finely diced (about 1 cup)
2 medium garlic cloves, thinly sliced
Kosher salt
2 tablespoons tomato paste
1 cup dry white wine
1 (28-ounce) can crushed San Marzano tomatoes
2 tablespoons honey
¼ cup red wine vinegar
Freshly ground black pepper
¾ cup finely chopped fresh dill

1. In a large pot, combine the beans with (unsalted) water to cover by at least 6 inches. Bring to a simmer over high heat, then reduce the heat to medium-low to maintain a gentle simmer. Partially cover and cook until the beans are just tender, about 30 minutes.

2. Meanwhile, set a large enameled Dutch oven over medium heat. Add the olive oil and heat to shimmering, then add the onions, carrots, garlic, and a pinch of salt. Cook, stirring occasionally, until the vegetables soften, about 5 minutes. Add the tomato paste and cook, stirring occasionally, until the paste begins to darken, about 1 minute. Add the wine and deglaze the pan, scraping with a wooden spoon to loosen the browned bits on the bottom of the pan. Cook until the wine reduces by half, about 2 minutes. Add the tomatoes, honey, and vinegar and cook until the tomato sauce thickens and reduces by one-third, about 10 minutes.

3. Reserving the cooking liquid, drain the beans. Add the beans and 1½ cups of the cooking liquid to the tomato sauce. Season to taste with salt and pepper. Cook until the beans are very tender, about 10 minutes. Remove from the heat and stir in the dill. Taste and adjust for seasoning, adding salt and pepper as needed.

MEATY PASTICCIO + GREEK VILLAGE SALAD

Serves 8 to 10

Well, hello childhood, I've missed you! Growing up, barely a week went by without a big portion of pasticcio landing in front of me, either at home or at a cousin's house. Not that I'm complaining! To me, this dish is a heartwarming taste of my youth. At the risk of offending my mom, I'd argue that my latest recipe is the best of them all—even hers! I'm sure it seems silly to try and arrange the pasta in the casserole so that the noodles are all lined up in the same direction, but it makes for such a killer presentation when it's sliced. (I promise it will taste just as good if you skip that step though.) And as for the salad, this is what comes to mind when I hear the phrase "Greek salad." It's ripped straight out of my mom's recipe box.

Meat Sauce

3 tablespoons extra-virgin olive oil
1 pound ground beef (80% lean)
1 pound ground lamb
Kosher salt and freshly ground black pepper
2 large yellow onions, diced (about 2 cups)
1 tablespoon whole fresh thyme leaves
½ teaspoon Aleppo pepper
½ teaspoon ground cinnamon
1 cup dry white wine
3 cups canned crushed tomatoes

Béchamel

8 tablespoons (1 stick) unsalted butter
½ cup all-purpose flour
½ teaspoon freshly grated nutmeg
4 cups whole milk
Kosher salt and freshly ground black pepper
1 cup finely grated kefalotyri or pecorino cheese
3 large eggs

Assembly and Serving

Extra-virgin olive oil, for the baking dish
Kosher salt
1 pound #1 macaroni (the long, straight tubes—not elbows)
4 tablespoons (½ stick) unsalted butter, melted
1 cup grated kefalotyri or pecorino cheese
Freshly ground black pepper
Greek Village Salad (page 45)

1. Make the meat sauce: Set a large Dutch oven over medium-high heat. Add the olive oil and heat to shimmering, then add the beef and lamb. Season with a pinch of salt and twist of black pepper. Cook, stirring with a wooden spoon to break up the meat, until well browned, about 10 minutes. Add the onions and cook, stirring occasionally, until they soften, about 3 minutes. Add the thyme, Aleppo, and cinnamon and cook until fragrant, about 30 seconds. Add the wine and deglaze the pan, scraping with a wooden spoon to loosen the browned bits on the bottom of the pan. Cook until the sauce reduces by half, about 2 minutes. Add the tomatoes and 1 cup water. Reduce the heat to medium-low to maintain a gentle simmer and cook until the tomatoes have begun to break down, about 30 minutes.

(recipe continues)

2. Meanwhile, make the béchamel: In a large saucepan, melt the butter over medium heat. Add the flour and cook, while whisking, for 1 minute. Add the nutmeg and, while constantly whisking, slowly add the milk. Cook, whisking occasionally, until smooth and thickened, about 4 minutes. Season with a pinch of salt and twist of black pepper. Remove from the heat, add the kefalotyri, and whisk until the cheese has melted. Add the eggs and whisk to blend. Cover and set aside.

3. Preheat the oven to 400°F. Line a sheet pan with parchment paper. Grease a 9 × 13-inch baking dish with olive oil.

4. Assemble the dish: Add 2 tablespoons salt to a medium pot of water and bring to a boil over high heat. Add the pasta and cook, stirring occasionally so it doesn't stick together, for 2 minutes less than the package directions. Drain the pasta, add it to a large bowl along with the melted butter and kefalotyri and toss to coat. Season with a pinch of salt and twist of black pepper.

5. Neatly arrange the pasta in the baking dish so that the noodles are all facing the same direction (yes, this takes patience, but it's worth it—and required!—for clean cuts). Add the meat sauce and smooth it out to an even layer with a spatula. Pour the béchamel evenly across the top and use the spatula to even it out.

6. Place the baking dish on the sheet pan and bake, uncovered, until the top is golden brown and puffy, about 45 minutes. Allow to cool for at least 30 minutes before slicing into squares.

7. Serve with the Greek salad.

(recipe continues)

Simply Symon Suppers

Greek Village Salad

Serves 8

4 tablespoons red wine vinegar
Juice of 2 lemons
2 medium garlic cloves, minced or grated
4 teaspoons finely chopped fresh oregano
4 teaspoons finely chopped fresh flat-leaf parsley
⅔ cup extra-virgin olive oil
Kosher salt and freshly ground black pepper
4 vine or heirloom tomatoes, cut into wedges

2 small English cucumbers, cut into 2-inch lengths and quartered lengthwise
2 red bell peppers, cut into large pieces
½ cup pitted kalamata olives
1 medium red onion, thinly sliced (about ⅓ cup)
1 (8-ounce) block Greek feta, broken into large chunks (about ½ cup)

1. In a medium bowl, whisk together the vinegar, lemon juice, garlic, oregano, parsley, and olive oil. Season with a pinch of salt and twist of pepper. Add the tomatoes, cucumbers, bell peppers, olives, and onion and toss to combine. Taste and adjust for seasoning, adding salt and pepper as needed.

2. Transfer the salad to a large platter and top with the feta.

CHICKEN CACCIATORE

+

CLASSIC RISOTTO

+

PEA GREENS CAESAR

Serves 4

Chicken cacciatore is a classic Italian American dish that packs a ton of flavor into every bite. I braise both white and dark meat chicken (can't say that I'm not a people pleaser!) in a tomato sauce loaded with aromatics. I serve the chicken on top of a classic, creamy risotto, which takes the dish to a whole new level. I know a lot of home cooks are anxious about making risotto, but it's super easy; it just requires patience and stirring. Start the risotto 20 minutes before the chicken is ready, saving some chicken stock for the very end so that the rice is a little on the loose side. I think the biggest mistake people make with risotto is serving it too dry and "tight." It should be liquidy enough to spread when placed on the platter—not stay frozen in a mound like mashed potatoes! The pea greens salad, served on the side, is the perfect springtime accompaniment. Store extra Caesar dressing in the refrigerator for up to 1 week.

2 pounds bone-in, skin-on chicken thighs
Kosher salt and freshly ground black pepper
2½ teaspoons ground fennel
1 tablespoon extra-virgin olive oil
¼ pound thick-sliced bacon, cut into ½-inch-long pieces
3 small portobello mushrooms, stemmed and gills removed, caps halved and thinly sliced (about 2 cups)
2 large yellow onions, finely chopped (about 2 cups)
2 stalks celery, finely chopped (about 1 cup)

1 cup diced carrots
½ cup olives
2 medium garlic cloves, minced
½ teaspoon crushed red pepper flakes
1 tablespoon finely chopped fresh rosemary
1 cup dry red wine
1 (28-ounce) can whole peeled tomatoes, preferably San Marzano
2 tablespoons finely chopped fresh flat-leaf parsley
Classic Risotto (opposite)
Pea Greens Caesar (page 50)

1. Set a large Dutch oven over medium-high heat. Season the chicken on all sides with salt, pepper, and 2 teaspoons of the ground fennel. Add the olive oil to the pan and heat to shimmering, then add the chicken thighs skin-side down. Cook until golden brown and crisp, about 5 minutes. Use tongs or a spatula to flip and continue cooking until the other side is also nicely browned, about 3 minutes. Transfer to a plate. Drain and discard the fat.

2. Set the pan back over medium-high heat and add the bacon. Cook, stirring occasionally, until it begins to get crispy, about 3 minutes. Add the mushrooms, onions, celery, carrots, olives, garlic, and a pinch of salt and continue to cook, stirring occasionally, until the vegetables soften, about 5 minutes. Add the remaining ½ teaspoon ground fennel, the pepper flakes, rosemary, and wine. Bring to a gentle boil and cook until the liquid is reduced by half, about 2 minutes.

3. Crush the tomatoes with your hands and add them to pan along with any liquid from the can. Return the chicken to the pan skin-side up, cover, and cook until the chicken reaches an internal temperature of 160°F, about 20 minutes. Remove from the heat and stir in the parsley.

4. Serve with the risotto and pea greens Caesar.

Classic Risotto

Serves 4

2 tablespoons extra-virgin
   olive oil
2 small yellow onions, finely
   chopped (about 1 cup)
Kosher salt
1 cup Arborio or Carnaroli rice

¾ cup dry white wine
4 cups chicken stock, warmed
1 tablespoon unsalted butter
⅓ cup finely grated parmesan
   cheese

1. Set a large skillet over medium heat. Add the olive oil and heat to shimmering, then add the onions and a pinch of salt. Cook, stirring occasionally, until the onion is soft, about 5 minutes.

2. Add the rice and cook, stirring constantly, for 1 minute. Add the wine and cook, stirring occasionally, until the wine has almost evaporated.

3. Add ½ cup of the chicken stock and cook, stirring constantly, until almost all of it has been absorbed by the rice. Repeat with ½-cup additions of stock, stirring constantly after each, until the stock is gone and the rice is tender, about 20 minutes. Make sure to reserve ½ cup stock for the very end to ensure a nice loose risotto

4. Remove from the heat, stir in the butter and parmesan, and serve.

(recipe continues)

Pea Greens Caesar

Serves 4

Caesar Dressing

1 medium garlic clove, peeled
2 large egg yolks
1½ teaspoons Worcestershire sauce
1 teaspoon Dijon mustard
¼ cup fresh lemon juice
¼ cup finely grated parmesan cheese
Kosher salt and freshly ground black pepper
½ cup extra-virgin olive oil

Bread Crumbs

4 cups ciabatta bread cubes
½ cup extra-virgin olive oil
Kosher salt and freshly ground black pepper

Salad

2 cups pea greens or watercress
2 cups thinly sliced snow peas
Freshly grated parmesan cheese, for serving (finely grated on a Microplane)
Freshly ground black pepper

1. Preheat the oven to 350°F.

2. Make the Caesar dressing: In a blender or food processor, combine the garlic, egg yolks, Worcestershire sauce, mustard, lemon juice, and parmesan and process until mostly smooth. Season with a pinch of salt and twist of pepper. With the machine running, slowly add the olive oil in a steady stream until the dressing is creamy. (Makes 1 cup of dressing.)

3. Make the bread crumbs: In a food processor, pulse the bread until it has the consistency of coarse crumbs (larger than panko but smaller than a crouton). Transfer to a medium bowl, add the olive oil, and season with a pinch of salt and twist of pepper. Mix well to fully coat the bread crumbs in oil. Arrange the bread crumbs on a sheet pan and bake, stirring halfway, until golden brown, about 20 minutes.

4. Assemble the salad: In a medium bowl, combine the pea greens and snow peas. Add dressing to taste and toss to coat. Transfer to a platter and top with the bread crumbs, additional parmesan, and black pepper.

GRANDMA PIE WITH MOZZ AND BASIL + ANTIPASTO SALAD

Serves 6

Everybody knows about thin-crust New York-style pizza, but true New Yorkers are also obsessed with "grandma pie." Like Sicilian pizza, grandma slices are rectangular in shape with a thick, tender base. After enjoying this style of pizza at home as a kid, in New York as an adult, and all over Rome while traveling, I set out to develop a recipe of my own. This is the one-hundredth version—give or take—of that dough, but I've finally nailed it. To me, the ideal grandma pie crust is crunchy yet still has an airy and buttery bite. A simple, delicious tomato sauce, plenty of tangy mozz, and fresh basil are the perfect toppers. To go with the pizza, I reach back to my favorite pizzeria-style salads loaded with deli meats, cheeses, chickpeas, and pepperoncini. After the dough has risen once, it can be refrigerated up to 3 days.

Pizza Dough

5 cups bread flour, plus more for rolling and shaping
2 tablespoons kosher salt
2 teaspoons active dry yeast or 6 teaspoons fresh yeast
2 cups lukewarm water (about 110°F)

Sauce

1 (28-ounce) can crushed San Marzano tomatoes
6 tablespoons extra-virgin olive oil
12 fresh basil leaves
3 medium garlic cloves, peeled
Kosher salt

Assembly and Serving

Extra-virgin olive oil, for the pans
12 ounces low-moisture mozzarella cheese (not fresh mozzarella), shredded
½ cup finely grated parmesan cheese
12 fresh whole basil leaves
Antipasto Salad (page 54)

1. Make the dough: In a stand mixer fitted with the dough hook, combine the flour, salt, and yeast. Blend on low while adding the lukewarm water. Continue blending on low until the dough comes together, about 2 minutes. Increase the speed to medium and knead until the dough is smooth and silky, about 10 minutes.

2. Turn the dough out onto a lightly floured surface and shape it into a tight ball. Return the dough to the mixer bowl, cover with plastic, and set in a warm spot to rise until doubled in size, about 1 hour.

3. Meanwhile, make the sauce: In a blender or food processor, combine the tomatoes, olive oil, basil, garlic, and a pinch of salt and process until smooth.

4. Position a rack in the center of the oven and preheat to 500°F.

5. Assemble the pizza: Divide the dough into 2 equal pieces. Grease two 9 × 13-inch sheet pans with olive oil. Place a piece into each pan and press it out to cover the entire bottom. Dividing evenly, top each pizza with the mozzarella, followed by the sauce. Bake until the crust is crispy and the cheese has melted, about 20 minutes.

6. Cut into rectangles, top with the parmesan and basil leaves, and serve with the antipasto salad.

(recipe continues)

Antipasto Salad

Serves 6

⅓ cup red wine vinegar
2 medium garlic cloves, minced or grated
2 tablespoons finely chopped fresh oregano
⅔ cup extra-virgin olive oil
Kosher salt and freshly ground black pepper
1 cup drained canned chickpeas
½ cup small-diced salami

½ cup small-diced aged provolone
½ cup halved cherry tomatoes
½ cup thinly sliced pepperoncini
4 cups shredded romaine lettuce (about 2 small heads)
6 tablespoons freshly grated parmesan cheese (finely grated on a Microplane), plus more for serving

1. In a screw-top jar, combine the vinegar, garlic, oregano, olive oil, a pinch of salt, and twist of pepper. Cover and shake vigorously to blend.

2. In a large bowl, combine the chickpeas, salami, provolone, tomatoes, pepperoncini, lettuce, and parmesan. Add dressing to taste, toss to combine, and top with freshly ground black pepper and more parmesan.

GNOCCHI WITH BROWN BUTTER, PEAS, AND MUSHROOMS

+

GRILLED ASPARAGUS AND LEMON

Serves 4

If you enjoy watching the Food Network, I'm sure you've heard Bobby Flay joke about how much I love to make gnocchi. Guilty! The dish is always one of the first things I think of making whether I'm cooking at home or competing in a studio kitchen. It's a food I keep going back to again and again because when they are made right, there simply is nothing better. This version, which I borrow from my Sicilian grandmother, is closer to a gnudi because it's made with ricotta. I prefer making them this way over the traditional potato version because they end up lighter, fluffier, and melt-in-your-mouth tender. To let the gnocchi truly shine, I finish them off with a heavenly brown butter and mushroom sauce. I like to serve it with lemony grilled asparagus topped with crispy parmesan bread crumbs for a little textural contrast.

Gnocchi

¾ cup all-purpose flour, plus more for shaping
½ cup freshly grated parmesan cheese (finely grated on a Microplane)
Grated zest of 1 lemon
¼ teaspoon kosher salt
1 cup whole-milk ricotta cheese
1 large egg

Assembly and Serving

2 tablespoons kosher salt, plus more to taste
1 tablespoon extra-virgin olive oil
2 cups mixed wild mushrooms, such as oyster, shiitake, and maitake, stems trimmed
1 cup fresh or frozen peas
Freshly ground black pepper
6 tablespoons unsalted butter
⅓ cup freshly grated parmesan cheese (finely grated on a Microplane)
Grilled Asparagus and Lemon (page 61)

1. Make the gnocchi: In a medium bowl, combine the flour, parmesan, lemon zest, and salt and whisk to combine. Add the ricotta and egg and stir with a wooden spoon or fork until the mixture just comes together, being careful to not overwork the dough. Turn the dough out onto a floured surface and press it into a rough square. With a bench scraper or knife, cut the dough into thirds. Using your palms and fingers, gently roll each piece out to ropes 1 inch thick and 12 inches long, adding flour as needed to prevent sticking. Cut the ropes crosswise into ½-inch-wide pieces.

2. To assemble: Set up an ice bath by filling a large bowl with ice and water. Add the salt to a medium pot of water and bring to a boil over high heat.

3. While waiting for the water to come to a boil, set a large skillet over medium-high heat. Add the olive oil and heat to shimmering. Add the mushrooms and shake the skillet to spread them out into an even layer. Cook, stirring minimally, until golden brown and crisp, about 5 minutes.

4. Once the water is at a boil, add the peas and cook until just al dente, about 1 minute. Use a slotted spoon to transfer the peas to the ice bath. Add the gnocchi to the boiling water and cook until they begin to float, about 2 minutes.

5. Add the blanched peas to the skillet with the mushrooms and season with salt and pepper. Add the butter and cook, stirring occasionally, until the butter begins to brown and smell nutty, about 2 minutes.

6. Using a slotted spoon, transfer the gnocchi from the pot of boiling water to the skillet. Add ¼ cup of the pasta water and gently stir to make a sauce. Remove from the heat and stir in the parmesan. Serve the gnocchi with the grilled asparagus and lemon.

Grilled Asparagus and Lemon

Serves 4

4 tablespoons extra-virgin
  olive oil
⅓ cup panko bread crumbs
Kosher salt
⅓ cup freshly grated parmesan
  cheese (finely grated on a
  Microplane)

1 pound thick green asparagus,
  woody ends trimmed
Freshly ground black pepper
1 lemon, halved

1. Set a large skillet over medium heat. Add 3 tablespoons of the olive oil and swirl to coat the bottom of the pan. Add the panko and shake the skillet to spread them out into an even layer. Cook, without stirring, until the edges begin to brown, about 2 minutes. Continue cooking, stirring, until the panko are evenly browned and toasted. Season with a pinch of salt and transfer to a bowl to cool. Once cool, stir in the parmesan.

2. Preheat an outdoor grill or grill pan to medium-high heat.

3. Drizzle the asparagus with the remaining 1 tablespoon olive oil and toss to coat. Season all sides with salt and pepper. Put the asparagus on the grill or grill pan and cook, using tongs to turn occasionally, until nicely charred on all sides, about 8 minutes. At the same time, place the lemon halves cut-side down on the grill or grill pan and cook, without moving, until nicely charred, about 8 minutes.

4. Transfer the asparagus to a plate, carefully squeeze the grilled lemon over top, and sprinkle with parmesan bread crumbs.

GRILLED
LAMB CHOPS
+
MINT SAUCE
+
LEMON
POTATOES
+
HORTA

Serves 4

Sometimes, the easiest preparation also happens to be the best. When it comes to bone-in lamb chops, I like a straightforward Greek-style marinade that goes heavy on the garlic and oregano followed by a quick sear on a hot grill. And if it's a wood or charcoal grill, all the better. A final drizzle of lemony mint sauce really makes the chops sing. If you've had and enjoyed Southern-style greens, think of horta as their Greek cousin. Loads of wholesome greens like kale, Swiss chard, and collards get cooked down with garlic, red onion, and fennel and finished with a bright pop of fresh dill. Rounding out the feast is a big batch of roasted Yukon Gold potatoes with a nice, lemony kick.

3 medium garlic cloves, grated
2 tablespoons finely chopped
   fresh oregano
Grated zest and juice of 1 lemon
2 teaspoons Dijon mustard
½ cup extra-virgin olive oil
Freshly ground black pepper

12 bone-in New Zealand lamb
   rib chops
Kosher salt
Mint Sauce (page 64)
Lemon Potatoes (page 64)
Horta (page 65)

1. In a large bowl, whisk together the garlic, oregano, lemon zest, lemon juice, mustard, and olive oil. Season with a few twists of black pepper. Add the lamb chops, tossing to coat all sides. Cover and refrigerate for 2 to 4 hours. Remove from the fridge 30 minutes before cooking.

2. Preheat a gas or charcoal grill to medium-high heat.

3. Remove the lamb from the marinade, allowing most of it to drip off. Reserve the excess marinade for basting. Season the lamb on all sides with salt. Grill the lamb until the bottom forms a nice crust, about 3 minutes. Baste the lamb with leftover marinade, flip, and continue cooking, while occasionally basting, until the other side is browned, about 3 minutes.

4. Remove from the grill and let rest, loosely tented with foil, for 5 minutes before serving. Serve with mint sauce, lemon potatoes, and horta.

> **Symon Says**
>
> You can make the mint sauce up to 1 day ahead of time if you want to get that out of the way. Then, start by making the horta, as it stays warm really well. Next move on to preparing the potatoes. While the potatoes are cooking, prepare the lamb.

(recipe continues)

Simply Symon Suppers

Mint Sauce

Makes 1¾ cups

1½ cups thinly sliced fresh mint
2 scallions, white and light-green parts only, thinly sliced (about ¼ cup)
2 medium garlic cloves, grated

Grated zest of ½ lemon plus the juice of 2 lemons
1 teaspoon Aleppo pepper
1½ cups extra-virgin olive oil
Pinch of kosher salt

In a medium bowl, whisk together the mint, scallions, garlic, lemon zest, lemon juice, Aleppo pepper, olive oil, and salt. Let stand for 30 minutes before serving.

Lemon Potatoes

Serves 4

6 medium Yukon Gold potatoes, scrubbed and quartered lengthwise
⅓ cup extra-virgin olive oil
1 teaspoon grated lemon zest plus ½ cup fresh lemon juice (2 to 3 lemons)

6 medium garlic cloves, unpeeled, smashed with the side of a knife
2 tablespoons Dijon mustard
6 sprigs fresh oregano
Kosher salt and freshly ground black pepper

1. Preheat the oven to 450°F.

2. In a large roasting pan, combine the potatoes, olive oil, lemon juice, garlic, mustard, oregano, and 1½ cups water and toss to combine. Season with a few pinches of salt and twists of pepper. Arrange the potatoes cut-side down and cook until they are just tender, about 35 minutes. Move the pan to the top third position in the oven.

3. Heat the broiler to high. Use a spatula to turn the potatoes so that the other cut side is down and broil until well browned, about 5 minutes.

4. Top with lemon zest and serve.

Horta

Serves 4

4 tablespoons extra-virgin olive oil
2 small red onions, halved and thinly sliced (about 1 cup)
3 medium garlic cloves, thinly sliced
1 large fennel bulb, halved, cored, and thinly sliced (about 2 cups)
Kosher salt
2 tablespoons tomato paste
1 pound lacinato kale, stemmed and sliced into 2-inch pieces
1 pound collard greens, stemmed and sliced into 2-inch pieces
1 pound Swiss chard, stems removed and thinly sliced, and leaves sliced into 2-inch pieces
Freshly ground black pepper
½ cup finely chopped fresh dill
Juice of 1 lemon

1. Set a large Dutch oven over medium heat. Add 2 tablespoons of the olive oil and the onions, garlic, and fennel. Season with a large pinch of salt and cook, stirring occasionally, until the vegetables soften, about 5 minutes.

2. Add the tomato paste and cook, stirring occasionally, until the paste begins to darken, about 1 minute. Add 1 cup water and deglaze the pan, scraping with a wooden spoon to loosen the browned bits on the bottom of the pan.

3. Add the kale, collard greens, and Swiss chard and stir to combine. If the greens don't all fit at first, cover the pan and let them cook down for 30 seconds, then add more. Season with a pinch of salt and twist of pepper. Add the remaining 2 tablespoons olive oil and cook, partially covered, stirring occasionally, until the greens are wilted, about 5 minutes.

4. Remove the pan from the heat and stir in the dill and lemon juice.

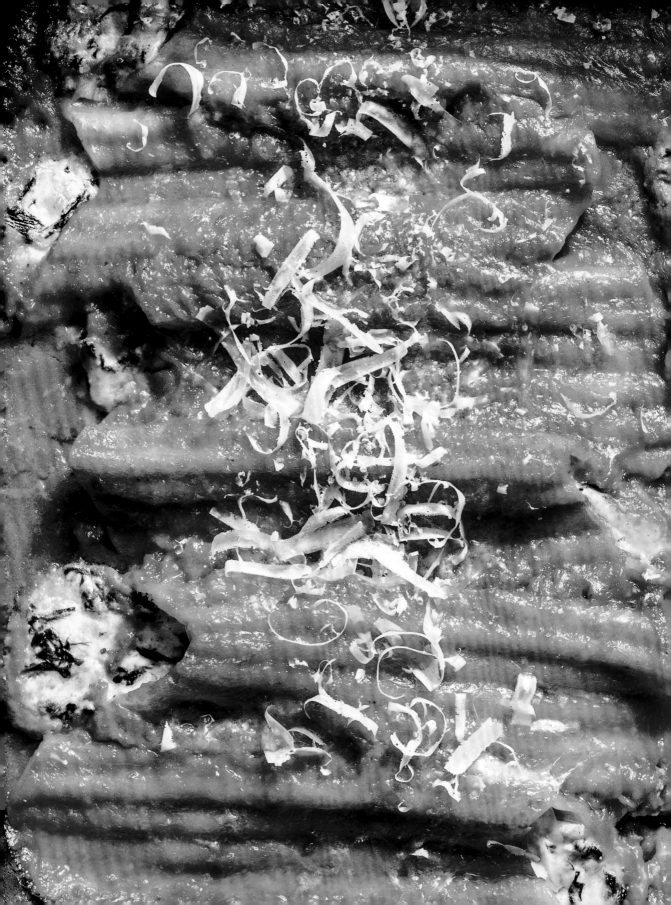

MANICOTTI STUFFED WITH RICOTTA AND SPINACH

+ SNAP PEA SALAD

Stuffed shells were not in the regular rotation in our family while growing up. But my mom did occasionally bust them out for big parties and important occasions, which is probably why they still feel special to me. It wasn't until I started making them myself that I realized how easy they were to assemble, especially using the technique in this recipe. Instead of delicately piping or spooning the savory ricotta and spinach filling into the long tubes, we simply cut the cooked pasta so it lies flat, fill them, and roll them. Genius, I know! Because it reheats so beautifully, manicotti is the perfect casserole to make ahead and bring to a party or potluck. I think it's much more impressive than your typical pasta bake. The springy snap pea salad is the perfect accompaniment, but this dish would also be amazing with the Greek Village Salad (page 45) or the Antipasto Salad (page 54).

Serves 4

Kosher salt
1 pound dried manicotti
2 tablespoons extra-virgin olive oil
2 medium garlic cloves, grated
1 (12-ounce) bag fresh spinach
Freshly ground black pepper
1 pound whole-milk ricotta cheese
1 cup shredded low-moisture mozzarella cheese

¾ cup freshly grated parmesan cheese (finely grated on a Microplane)
1 large egg, beaten
Grated zest of ½ lemon
½ teaspoon freshly grated nutmeg
Pomodoro Sauce (page 174)
Snap Pea Salad (page 70)

1. Add 2 tablespoons salt to a medium pot of water and bring to a boil over high heat.

2. Meanwhile, in a 9 × 13-inch baking dish, arrange the dried manicotti in an even layer.

3. Pour enough of the salted boiling water over the pasta to cover it by a few inches. Cover tightly with foil and let stand for 15 minutes. Drain the pasta in a colander, rinse under cold water, drain, and set aside. Reserve the baking dish for later.

4. Set a large saucepan over low heat. Add the olive oil followed by the garlic and cook until aromatic, about 1 minute. Add the spinach and cook, stirring occasionally, until the greens are wilted. If the greens don't all fit at first, add them in batches, waiting for one batch to wilt before adding the next. Season with a pinch of salt and twist of pepper. When all the spinach is wilted, transfer it to a colander to drain and cool. When cool enough to handle, squeeze out any remaining moisture and roughly chop.

5. In a large bowl, mix the ricotta, mozzarella, ½ cup of the parmesan, the

egg, lemon zest, nutmeg, and spinach. Lightly season with salt and pepper and stir to combine.

6. Preheat the oven to 400°F.

7. Spread ¾ cup of the pomodoro sauce evenly over the bottom of the 9 × 13-inch baking dish. Use kitchen shears to cut open each manicotti so it lies flat. Working with one piece at a time, arrange a small portion of the cheese mixture along one edge and roll the pasta to form a stuffed tube. Place seam-side down in the sauce. Repeat until all the pasta is filled and placed in the sauce. Evenly spread the rest of the pomodoro sauce on top of the manicotti. Sprinkle the remaining ¼ cup parmesan on top.

8. Loosely cover with foil and bake until the filling is warmed through and the pasta is tender, about 30 minutes. Remove the foil and continue to bake until the cheese filling is bubbling and the topping is golden brown, about 10 minutes.

9. Let stand for 5 minutes before serving with the snap pea salad.

(recipe continues)

Snap Pea Salad

Serves 4

4 tablespoons extra-virgin olive oil

8 ounces finely chopped pancetta (about 1 cup)

8 ounces snap peas or snow peas, thinly sliced lengthwise (about 2 cups)

4 scallions, white and light-green parts only, thinly sliced (about ½ cup)

4 ounces pea tendrils

½ cup thinly sliced fresh mint leaves

2 tablespoons fresh lemon juice

Kosher salt and freshly ground black pepper

3 ounces parmesan cheese, shaved with a vegetable peeler (about 1 cup)

1. Line a plate with paper towels. Set a large skillet over medium heat. Add 1 tablespoon of the olive oil and heat to shimmering, then add the pancetta and cook, stirring occasionally, until crisp, about 5 minutes. Transfer to the paper towels to drain.

2. In a large bowl, combine the snap peas, scallions, pea tendrils, and mint and toss to combine. Add the lemon juice and remaining 3 tablespoons olive oil. Season with a pinch of salt and twist of pepper. Garnish with the browned pancetta and shaved parmesan.

BRAISED BEEF STEW
+
SMASHED PEAS
+
GRILLED RED ONION SALAD

Serves 6

Spring in the Midwest has a habit of going from warm to cold, sun to snow, in the blink of an eye. On those unseasonably chilly days and nights, I lean into rich braises like this classic beef stew fortified with baby new potatoes. By pairing it with peas (preferably fresh, but frozen works, too), you can still cook with the seasons and add some brightness. I like to use the smashed peas as a creamy base for the stew. The salad manages to bridge the seasons as well by featuring grilled onions and radicchio, which add a woodsy sweetness. If you happen to be blessed with "Cleveland weather" on the day you're making this, swap the gas or charcoal grill for a stovetop grill pan when making the onion salad. You'll lose some smoky-charred goodness, but at least you won't get frostbite!

½ cup all-purpose flour
Kosher salt and freshly ground
   black pepper
1½ pounds boneless beef chuck
   roast, cut into large cubes
2 tablespoons extra-virgin
   olive oil
8 whole peeled small shallots
4 medium carrots, sliced
   (about 2 cups)
2 celery stalks, diced (about
   1 cup)
1 tablespoon tomato paste

2 tablespoons chopped fresh
   oregano
1 pound baby new potatoes,
   unpeeled, scrubbed
2 cups dry white wine
4 cups low-sodium chicken stock
2 fresh or dried bay leaves
3 large strips of lemon zest
1 tablespoon Dijon mustard
½ cup roughly chopped fresh
   tarragon
Smashed Peas (page 74)
Grilled Red Onion Salad
   (page 74)

1. Place the flour in a large bowl and season lightly with salt and pepper. Season the beef on all sides with salt and pepper. Dredge the beef in the seasoned flour, making sure to coat all sides well. Shake off the excess.

2. Set a large Dutch oven over medium-high heat. Add the olive oil and heat to shimmering, then add half the beef. Cook until golden brown on all sides, about 12 minutes. Use a slotted spoon to transfer to a plate when done. Repeat the process with the remaining beef.

3. To the same pan, add the shallots, carrots, celery, and a large pinch of salt. Cook, stirring occasionally, until the vegetables soften and begin to brown, about 3 minutes. Add the tomato paste and oregano and stir for 30 seconds. Add the potatoes, wine, chicken stock, bay leaves, lemon strips, and browned beef (and any accumulated juices). Bring to a boil, then reduce the heat to medium-low to maintain a gentle simmer, partially cover, and cook, stirring occasionally, until the potatoes and beef are tender, about 1 hour.

4. Remove from the heat and stir in the mustard and tarragon. Remove and discard the lemon strips and bay leaves before serving with the peas and grilled onion salad.

(recipe continues)

Smashed Peas

Serves 6

2 tablespoons unsalted butter
1 medium shallot, finely chopped
Kosher salt
2 cups fresh or frozen peas (if frozen, leave on the counter for 30 minutes to thaw)

Freshly ground black pepper
Grated zest of ½ lemon
¼ cup crème fraîche

1. In a medium saucepan, melt the butter over medium heat. Add the shallot and a pinch of salt and cook, stirring occasionally, until the shallots are soft, about 2 minutes.

2. Add the peas and ¼ cup water, cover, and cook until the peas are warmed through, about 5 minutes. Remove from the heat and roughly mash the peas with a potato masher, leaving some texture. Season with a pinch of salt and twist of pepper. Stir in the lemon zest and crème fraîche and serve.

Grilled Red Onion Salad

Serves 6

1 large red onion, sliced into 1-inch-thick rings
2 heads radicchio, cored and quartered
½ cup extra-virgin olive oil, plus more for drizzling

Kosher salt and freshly ground black pepper
3 tablespoons red wine vinegar
2 teaspoons whole-grain mustard
⅓ cup crumbled blue cheese
⅓ cup chopped fresh flat-leaf parsley

1. Preheat a gas or charcoal grill for indirect cooking, with one hot side and one hold (unheated) side.

2. Arrange the onion and radicchio on a sheet pan or grill basket, drizzle with olive oil (I use about 1 tablespoon), and season with a few pinches of salt and twists of black pepper. Put the pan on the hot side of the grill and cook, flipping the vegetables halfway, until nicely charred on both sides, about 3 minutes. If the onions are not tender, move the pan to the hold side, cover the grill, and continue cooking for 3 minutes.

3. In a small bowl, whisk together the vinegar, mustard, and the ½ cup olive oil. Season with a pinch of salt and twist of pepper.

4. Arrange the onions and radicchio on the bottom of a platter, dress to taste with vinaigrette, and top with the blue cheese and parsley.

ROASTED SALMON
+
SHAVED CUCUMBERS AND RADISHES
+
CREAMY DILL SAUCE

Serves 4 to 6

When I'm looking for something easy, healthy, and satisfying, I keep returning to salmon. It has such a rich, meaty texture—and it responds well to every form of cooking. Here, the fish gets a quick sweet-and-sour marinade before roasting on a sheet pan in a hot oven. In the spring, my garden and nearby farmers' markets are brimming with fresh, crunchy radishes, so we combine them with cukes for a refreshing side salad. You can serve the creamy dill sauce on the side, but I prefer to serve the salmon right on top of a pool of it so all the juices and flavors mingle together in joyous harmony.

1 cup freshly squeezed orange juice (about 3 medium oranges)
Juice of 1 lemon
½ cup pure maple syrup
2 medium garlic cloves, grated
1 tablespoon grated fresh ginger
½ teaspoon crushed red pepper flakes
2-pound side skin-on wild salmon, pin bones removed
Kosher salt and freshly ground black pepper
Creamy Dill Sauce (page 78)
2 scallions, white and light-green parts only, thinly sliced (about ¼ cup)
Shaved Cucumbers and Radishes (page 78)

1. In a medium bowl, whisk together the orange juice, lemon juice, maple syrup, garlic, ginger, and pepper flakes. Transfer to a 9 × 13-inch baking dish. Add the fish flesh-side down and marinate at room temperature for 30 minutes.

2. Preheat the oven to 450°F. Line a sheet pan with parchment paper.

3. Remove the fish from the marinade, allowing most of it to drip off. Place the salmon skin-side down on the sheet pan. Transfer the remaining marinade to a small saucepan.

4. While the oven preheats, set the saucepan of marinade over medium heat and bring to a boil, then reduce the heat to medium-low to maintain a gentle simmer and cook, stirring occasionally, until it has thickened to a glaze, about 20 minutes.

5. Season the fish with a pinch of salt and twist of pepper and roast until the fish turns light pink and begins to firm up, about 10 minutes. Brush the glaze evenly over the fish and continue cooking until the fish is firm and completely cooked through and the glaze becomes sticky, about 6 minutes.

6. Let stand for 5 minutes before portioning and serving. Spoon a pool of dill sauce on a plate and top with a portion of salmon (or serve the sauce on the side). Garnish the salmon with the scallions and serve the cucumber and radish salad on the side.

(recipe continues)

Shaved Cucumbers and Radishes

Serves 4 to 6

2 tablespoons sherry vinegar
2 tablespoons Dijon mustard
1 teaspoon sugar
¼ cup extra-virgin olive oil
1 medium English cucumber, thinly sliced (about 2 cups)
1 pound radishes, thinly sliced (about 2 cups)
4 scallions, white and light-green parts only, thinly sliced (about ½ cup)
¼ cup chopped fresh flat-leaf parsley
Kosher salt and freshly ground black pepper

In a small bowl, whisk together the vinegar, Dijon mustard, sugar, and olive oil. Add the cucumber, radishes, scallions, and parsley. Season with a pinch of salt and twist of pepper and toss to combine. Let stand for 5 minutes before serving.

Creamy Dill Sauce

Makes 1 cup

1 cup sour cream
2 tablespoons prepared horseradish
1 medium garlic clove, grated
¼ cup finely chopped fresh dill
3 teaspoons white wine vinegar
Kosher salt and freshly ground black pepper

In a medium bowl, combine all the ingredients, season with a pinch of salt and twist of pepper, and whisk to combine.

Sunny Days, Cool Nights

Hot and Easygoing

As an avid gardener, summer will always hold a special place in my heart. I often begin my days just wandering through the backyard, enjoying the peace and quiet and taking in all the ripening herbs, fruits, and veggies that are coming into their own. There are few greater joys than popping a sweet and juicy cherry tomato — still warm from the sun and picked right off the vine — into your mouth. This is also when I typically plan my meals, taking note of what's ready to be harvested and transformed into a salad, side dish, or even main course. Growing up, I felt the same sense of excitement when we would stop at our favorite roadside farm stand for some ripe blackberries, crisp green beans, or my all-time favorite: freshly picked Ohio sweet corn.

In summer, my grills and smokers are usually going nonstop. I tend to do the majority of my cooking outdoors — preferably cold beer in hand. This chapter is filled with easygoing recipes like Whole Grilled Snapper (page 85), Grilled Salmon Steaks (page 117), and Smoked Pulled Pork (page 98). The same goes for the side dishes, which are often grilled, charred, or fire-roasted. When the produce is this fresh and flavorful, the key is to allow them to shine by doing as little as possible. It's amazing how a few minutes over a hot fire brings out the natural sweetness in vegetables while adding layers of complexity and depth.

This chapter is probably the most flexible one when it comes to moving recipes around. Pretty much every side dish and salad can be paired with any of the proteins and vice versa. Also, if you're entertaining or expecting a few extra guests, these recipes scale up with ease.

WHOLE GRILLED SNAPPER
+
GRILL-ROASTED TOMATOES
+
ANCHOVY BREAD

Serves 4

Living by the water in New York, I'm fortunate to be close to people who love to fish. I'm even more thankful that I can call many of those people my friends! Whenever I'm gifted a pristine freshly caught fish like a snapper, the last thing I want to do is mess with it too much. That means gutting it, scaling it, seasoning it, and cooking it whole. Not only is this the easiest way to cook most fish, it also results in the juiciest and most delicious flesh, because the bones add flavor while keeping it moist. To evenly cook the fish all the way through regardless of its thickness, sear it on both sides over the hot side of the grill and then slide it over to the unheated side to finish. I could make an entire meal of this grilled anchovy bread, which gets topped with roasted tomatoes—a great trick for coaxing a lot of sweetness from a grocery store tomato. It's like a little taste of Spain in my own backyard.

1½ cups extra-virgin olive oil, plus extra for grilling
Grated zest of 3 lemons plus ½ cup fresh lemon juice (2 to 3 lemons)
3 medium garlic cloves, minced
2 cups fresh flat-leaf parsley, finely chopped
1 shallot, minced

1 jalapeño, seeded and minced
Kosher salt and freshly ground black pepper
1 whole snapper (3 to 4 pounds), cleaned and scaled
Grill-Roasted Tomatoes (page 86)
Anchovy Bread (page 86)

1. In a medium bowl, whisk together the olive oil, lemon zest, lemon juice, garlic, parsley, shallot, and jalapeño. Season the lemon marinade with a pinch of salt and twist of pepper.

2. Make three slashes ½ inch deep and 2 to 3 inches long into each side of the fish, spacing them about 1 inch apart. Liberally apply half of the lemon marinade to both sides of the fish, making sure to get it deep into the slashes. Reserve the remaining marinade for later. Cover with plastic wrap and refrigerate for 2 to 4 hours.

3. Preheat a gas or charcoal grill for indirect cooking, with one hot side and one hold (unheated) side. Remove the fish from the refrigerator. Brush a grill basket with olive oil.

4. Season the fish on both sides with a few pinches of salt and twists of pepper. Place it in the grill basket, set on the hot side of the grill, and cook until nicely charred, about 8 minutes. Flip and cook until the second side is nicely charred, about 8 minutes longer. (Using an instant-read thermometer, you're looking for about 140°F at the thickest part.) If the fish is burning or charring too quickly, move it to the hold side of the grill to finish cooking.

5. Transfer the fish to a platter, top with reserved marinade, and serve with the grilled tomatoes and anchovy bread topped with roasted tomatoes, if desired.

(recipe continues)

Grill-Roasted Tomatoes

Serves 4

4 medium vine tomatoes
2 tablespoons extra-virgin
  olive oil
2 tablespoons red wine vinegar

1 tablespoon finely chopped fresh
  oregano
Kosher salt and freshly ground
  black pepper
Flaky sea salt, for serving

1. Preheat a gas or charcoal grill for indirect cooking, with one hot side and one hold (unheated) side.

2. Put the whole tomatoes on the hold side of the grill, cover the grill, and cook until the skins begin to blister and soften, about 25 minutes (there's no need to turn the tomatoes since they're on the indirect heat side).

3. Meanwhile, in a small bowl, whisk together the olive oil, vinegar, and oregano. Season with a pinch of kosher salt and twist of pepper.

4. Transfer the tomatoes to a platter, drizzle with vinaigrette, garnish with flaky salt, and serve.

Anchovy Bread

Serves 4

Small loaf of rustic bread, cut into
  4 thick (¾-inch) slices
2 tablespoons extra-virgin
  olive oil
Kosher salt and freshly ground
  black pepper

1 medium garlic clove, peeled
12 oil-packed whole white
  anchovies
½ cup fresh flat-leaf parsley
  leaves

1. Preheat an outdoor grill or grill pan to medium-high heat.

2. Brush both sides of the bread slices with the olive oil, season with a few pinches of salt and twists of pepper, and place on the grill. Cook until slightly charred and toasted on both sides, about 30 seconds per side.

3. While the bread is still warm, rub each slice with the garlic clove until aromatic.

4. Top each slice with 3 anchovies and a layer of parsley leaves.

STICKY PORK RIBS + COCONUT RICE + PAPAYA RELISH

Serves 4

Typically, I am a no-sauce kind of guy when it comes to my barbecue. But I make an exception for these finger-licking ribs. These are basted with Kansas City-style barbecue sauce until the glaze becomes sticky-sweet on the grill. Wait until the last hour of cooking to begin basting, otherwise the sugars in the sauce will burn before the ribs are cooked through. I like to put a little of the fruity, tropical papaya relish right on top of my ribs and serve it all with Lizzie's famous coconut rice.

½ cup kosher salt
½ cup butcher-grind black pepper
1 tablespoon sweet paprika
2 teaspoons celery seeds
2 teaspoons ground coriander
2 (3- to 4-pound) slabs pork spareribs

Applewood chips for smoking (about 4 handfuls)
Kansas City BBQ Sauce (page 91) or your favorite store-bought barbecue sauce
Coconut Rice (page 90)
Papaya Relish (page 90)

1. In a medium bowl, combine the salt, pepper, paprika, celery seeds, and coriander.

2. Slide a butter knife under a corner of the thin white membrane on the bone side of the spareribs to free it from the meat. Using a paper towel for grip, peel off the entire membrane and discard it. Pat the ribs dry with paper towels and season on both sides with the rub.

3. Prepare a charcoal grill with the "snake method" by mounding and overlapping three or four unlit briquettes on the bottom charcoal grate around the perimeter of the grill base. Place wood chips or chunks on top of the unlit coals at regular intervals to generate smoke throughout the entire process. Light a chimney half-filled with charcoal. When burning white-hot, carefully pour the coals onto one end of the briquette circle to ignite the snake.

4. When the temperature in the grill reaches 300°F, put the ribs bone-side down in the center of the grill. After 2½ hours, test the ribs for doneness by flipping a rack and pressing the meat between the bones. If the meat pulls away from the bones, it's done. If not, continue smoking until it does, about 30 minutes more, checking every 10 minutes or so. During the last hour of cooking, baste the meat side of the ribs with BBQ sauce every 20 minutes.

5. When the ribs are done, gently brush them with more sauce, being careful not to remove the beautiful bark that forms on the exterior of the meat. Cut between the bones to serve.

6. Serve the ribs with more barbecue sauce, the coconut rice, and papaya relish.

(recipe continues)

Coconut Rice

Serves 4

2 cups jasmine rice
1 (13-ounce) can full-fat coconut milk
1 medium garlic clove, grated

Grated zest of 1 lime
1 teaspoon kosher salt
⅓ cup finely chopped fresh cilantro

1. Place the rice in a fine-mesh sieve and rinse under cold water until the water runs clear. Place the rice in medium bowl, add cold water to cover by a few inches, and set aside for 15 minutes. Drain and rinse the rice.

2. In a medium saucepan, combine the coconut milk, ½ cup water, the garlic, lime zest, salt, and rice and stir to combine. Bring to a boil over medium heat, then reduce the heat to medium-low to maintain a gentle simmer. Cover and cook until the rice is tender and the liquid is absorbed, about 15 minutes. Remove from the heat and let stand covered for 10 minutes.

3. Sprinkle on the cilantro, fluff with a fork, and serve.

Papaya Relish

Makes 2½ cups

2 cups finely chopped papaya
2 scallions, white and light-green parts only, thinly sliced (about ¼ cup)
¼ cup finely chopped fresh cilantro

1 tablespoon finely chopped seeded jalapeño
2 tablespoons fresh lime juice
1 teaspoon Aleppo pepper
Kosher salt

In a medium bowl, combine the papaya, scallions, cilantro, jalapeño, lime juice, and Aleppo pepper and toss to combine. Season with salt to taste.

Kansas City BBQ Sauce

Makes 3 cups

3 tablespoons extra-virgin olive oil
1 small yellow onion, finely chopped
3 garlic cloves, minced
Kosher salt
2 cups tomato sauce
¼ cup tomato paste

½ cup brown sugar
⅓ cup dark molasses
⅓ cup apple cider vinegar
3 tablespoons yellow mustard
1 tablespoon chili powder
½ teaspoon cayenne pepper
Freshly ground black pepper

1. Set a medium nonreactive saucepan over medium heat. Add the olive oil and heat to shimmering, then add the onion, garlic, and a pinch of salt. Cook, stirring occasionally, until the vegetables soften, about 5 minutes. Reduce the heat to medium-low, add the tomato sauce, tomato paste, brown sugar, molasses, vinegar, mustard, chili powder, and cayenne and whisk to combine. Season with a few pinches of salt and twists of black pepper. Bring to a gentle simmer and cook, stirring occasionally, until the flavors come together, about 30 minutes. Carefully transfer the sauce to a blender or food processer and puree until smooth.

2. Use immediately or store in the refrigerator in an airtight container for up to 2 weeks or the freezer for up to 1 month.

SWORDFISH KEBABS

\+

RADISH CUCUMBER SALAD

\+

LEMON YOGURT SAUCE

Serves 4

This is such a great recipe for two people or twenty people (you'd have to scale it up, obviously). I am doing this with swordfish, but any firm steak-cut fish would work great with this marinade, such as tuna, halibut, or mahimahi, as would boneless, skinless chicken thighs or pork tenderloin. When grilling, try and get in the habit of setting up a two-zone grill, with a hot (direct) and less-hot (indirect) side so you can sear the fish (or meats) and then finish them over more moderate heat. I could literally drink the lemon yogurt sauce out of a cup, it's that good. Use it as a base, a topper, or dip for the kebabs. Urfa pepper is one my new favorite spices because it adds a smoky-sweet kick to foods. If you can't track it down, swap in an equal amount of crushed red pepper flakes, cayenne pepper, chili powder, or Aleppo pepper.

2 pounds skinless swordfish steaks, cut into 1½-inch cubes
1 cup extra-virgin olive oil
⅓ cup whole-milk Greek yogurt
¼ cup fresh lemon juice
2 medium garlic cloves, grated
2 teaspoons dried oregano
1 teaspoon ground cumin
1½ teaspoons Urfa pepper
1½ teaspoons kosher salt

1 teaspoon coarsely ground black pepper
Vegetable oil, for the grill grates
4 (12-inch) skewers, soaked in water for at least 30 minutes if using wood
Lemon Yogurt Sauce (page 94)
Radish Cucumber Salad (page 94)

1. Place the swordfish in a 1-gallon zip-top bag.

2. In a large bowl, whisk together the olive oil, yogurt, lemon juice, garlic, oregano, cumin, Urfa pepper, salt, and black pepper. Pour over the swordfish and marinate in the refrigerator for 1 to 2 hours.

3. Preheat a gas or charcoal grill to high heat. When hot, oil the grill grates to prevent sticking.

4. Remove the swordfish from the bag, allowing most of the marinade to drip off (discard the marinade). Thread 4 or 5 pieces of fish onto each of four skewers, grouping them near the top so that the tip is covered by the meat.

5. Set the skewers on the grill and cook until lightly charred on all sides and cooked through, about 3 minutes per side.

6. Transfer the kebabs to a platter or plates. Drizzle on the lemon yogurt sauce or serve it on the side for dipping. Serve the radish cucumber salad alongside.

(recipe continues)

Lemon Yogurt Sauce

Makes 2 cups

1½ cups whole-milk Greek yogurt
½ cup extra-virgin olive oil
Grated zest of 1 lemon
2 tablespoons fresh lemon juice
1 teaspoon Urfa pepper
2 scallions, white and light-green parts only, thinly sliced (about ¼ cup)
Kosher salt and freshly ground black pepper

In a medium bowl, combine the yogurt, olive oil, lemon zest, lemon juice, Urfa pepper, and scallions. Season with a pinch of salt and twist of black pepper and whisk to combine.

Radish Cucumber Salad

Serves 4

½ cup extra-virgin olive oil
¼ cup white wine vinegar
2 medium garlic cloves, grated
Kosher salt and freshly ground black pepper
10 to 12 medium to large radishes, sliced paper thin (preferably using a mandoline; about 2 cups)
2 medium cucumbers, peeled and thinly sliced (about 2 cups)
1 small red onion, halved and thinly sliced (about ½ cup)
2 tablespoons finely chopped fresh dill

In a medium bowl, whisk together the olive oil, vinegar, and garlic. Season with a pinch of salt and twist of pepper. Add the radishes, cucumbers, onion, and dill and gently toss to combine.

GRILLED SKIRT STEAK WITH ROMESCO SAUCE + TOASTED BREAD SALAD

Serves 4

Yes, the rib eye is the undisputed king of steak cuts, but if I had to choose another that's nearly as delicious and a whole lot more flexible, it would be the skirt steak. Not only is the cut super beefy in flavor, it's also a fraction of the price and appropriate for so many recipes. (Tacos, anyone?!) Make sure you slice the steak crosswise and against the grain before topping it with the romesco sauce, which adds an earthy, sweet, nutty complexity. The toasted bread salad is an explosion of flavors and textures that marry perfectly with the romesco sauce. The vinaigrette gets a big boost from the addition of smoked paprika.

¼ cup plus 1 tablespoon extra-virgin olive oil
4 large garlic cloves, smashed and peeled
½ cup Marcona almonds
1 (12-ounce) jar piquillo peppers, drained

2 tablespoons sherry vinegar
Kosher salt
1 (2-pound) skirt steak
Freshly ground black pepper
Toasted Bread Salad (page 97)

1. Set a large saucepan over medium-low heat. Add ¼ cup of the olive oil and heat to shimmering, then add the garlic and cook, stirring occasionally, until it softens and begins to brown, about 4 minutes. Add the almonds and cook, stirring occasionally, until the nuts are lightly toasted, about 2 minutes. Add the peppers, vinegar, and a large pinch of salt and cook for 3 minutes. Carefully transfer to a blender or food processer and blend until smooth. Taste and adjust for seasoning, adding salt as needed. Set aside half the romesco sauce for serving.

2. Pierce the skirt steak with a fork or paring knife a few times on both sides. Place the steak in a 1-gallon zip-top bag. Pour the other half of the sauce over the steak and refrigerate for 1 to 4 hours.

3. Preheat an outdoor grill or grill pan to medium-high heat. Remove the steak from the refrigerator and set aside to come to room temperature while the grill heats (or take out from the fridge 15 to 20 minutes before heating the pan). Remove the steak from the bag, allowing most of the marinade to drip off (discard the marinade).

4. Using paper towels, pat the steak dry. Drizzle the steak with the remaining 1 tablespoon olive oil and season both sides with salt and pepper. Place the steak on the grill and cook, without moving, until nicely charred, about 4 minutes. Flip and continue cooking until medium-rare, about 4 minutes. Set aside to rest, loosely tented with foil, for 5 minutes before slicing against the grain.

5. To serve, spoon the reserved romesco sauce onto a platter, top with the sliced steak, and serve with the toasted bread salad.

(recipe continues)

Toasted Bread Salad

Serves 4

6 tablespoons extra-virgin olive oil
Kosher salt and freshly ground black pepper
6 (1-inch-thick) slices ciabatta bread, torn into 1-inch cubes
3 tablespoons sherry vinegar
2 medium garlic cloves, grated
½ teaspoon smoked paprika
1 teaspoon honey

3 vine tomatoes, cored and quartered
3 cups baby arugula
1 (12-ounce) jar piquillo peppers, drained and roughly chopped
⅔ cup Marcona almonds
8 ounces blue cheese, preferably Spanish, broken into large pieces

1. Preheat the oven to 350°F.

2. In a large bowl, combine 2 tablespoons of the olive oil, a pinch of salt, and a twist of pepper. Add the bread cubes and toss to evenly coat. Arrange the bread in an even layer on a sheet pan and toast until golden brown, about 15 minutes.

3. Meanwhile, in the same bowl, whisk together the remaining 4 tablespoons olive oil, the vinegar, garlic, smoked paprika, and honey. Season with a pinch of salt and a twist of pepper. Add the tomatoes and arugula and toss to combine.

4. Place the toasted bread on a platter, top with the tomato and arugula salad, and garnish with the chopped piquillo peppers, whole almonds, and chunks of blue cheese.

SMOKED PULLED PORK
+
LIZ'S BISCUITS
+
CABBAGE AND CARROT SLAW

Serves 6

If you're new to the barbecue game, smoked pork shoulder is a wonderful place to start. Out of all the meats and cuts, pork shoulder (also called pork butt) is one of the most forgiving because the large amount of internal fat keeps the meat moist during cooking. While low and slow in a real wood smoker is the preferred cooking method, this pork will still be a crowd-pleaser if cooked in a moderate oven. When you pair the pulled pork with a classic cabbage and carrot slaw and Liz's heavenly buttermilk biscuits, you get the ultimate summer picnic. Bonus points for the smart folks who stack that tender pork and crunchy slaw into a split biscuit and call it a sammy! To quickly grind whole peppercorns, add them to a clean coffee grinder or pulverize in a small food processor.

½ cup kosher salt
2 tablespoons light or dark brown sugar
Applewood chips for smoking (about 4 handfuls)
¼ cup coarsely ground black pepper
1 tablespoon celery seeds
1 tablespoon ground coriander
1 tablespoon sweet paprika

1 (4- to 6-pound) bone-in pork shoulder
1 cup apple cider
¼ cup hot honey (or ¼ cup honey with a few splashes of hot sauce to taste)
Liz's Biscuits (page 101)
Cabbage and Carrot Slaw (page 102)

1. This step is for those who have a meat injector. If you don't have one, move to step 2. In a medium saucepan, bring 1 cup water to a simmer over medium-high heat. Add ¼ cup of the salt and the brown sugar and whisk until completely dissolved. Remove from the heat, add 1 cup cold water, and stir to combine. Fill a 2-ounce injector with brine and inject the pork with brine on all sides. Discard any unused brine.

2. Preheat a smoker to 225°F. Add a handful of applewood chips to the smoker.

3. In a medium bowl, stir together the remaining ¼ cup salt, the pepper, celery seeds, coriander, and paprika. Season the pork liberally on all sides with the rub.

4. When the temperature in the smoker reaches 225°F and the smoke is running clear, add the pork and cook until the meat reaches an internal temperature of 195°F, about 6 to 8 hours. Add a handful of wood chips every hour for the first 4 hours. An hour or so before the pork is finished cooking, combine the apple cider and honey and baste the mixture all over the meat every 15 minutes until the pork is up to temp.

5. Use heat-resistant gloves to transfer the pork to a cutting board and let rest for 10 minutes before pulling or shredding the meat. Serve with the biscuits and slaw.

(recipe continues)

Liz's Biscuits

Makes 7 biscuits

2 cups all-purpose flour, plus more for shaping
2 teaspoons baking powder
½ teaspoon baking soda
1 teaspoon kosher salt

8 tablespoons (1 stick) cold unsalted butter, cut into ½-inch pieces
1 cup cold full-fat buttermilk or unsweetened kefir

1. Position a rack in the center of the oven and preheat to 425°F. Line a sheet pan with parchment paper.

2. In a large bowl, whisk together the flour, baking powder, baking soda, and salt to blend. Add the cold butter and cut it in using a pastry cutter or your fingers until you have a coarse crumb (the butter pieces should be no bigger than a pea) and the butter is fully coated. Place the bowl in the freezer for 10 minutes.

3. Remove the flour-butter mixture from the freezer, make a well in the center, and add the buttermilk. With a wooden spoon, gently stir until the mixture comes together into a shaggy dough.

4. Turn the dough out onto a lightly floured surface and press to a 1-inch thickness. Flour a 2½-inch biscuit cutter and cut out the biscuits by pressing straight down without twisting. Place the biscuits on the prepared sheet pan, leaving space between them. Bake until golden brown and flaky, about 15 minutes. Serve warm.

(recipe continues)

Cabbage and Carrot Slaw

Serves 6

½ cup mayonnaise (Duke's or
  Hellmann's)
¼ cup white wine vinegar
1 tablespoon sugar
Kosher salt and freshly ground
  black pepper

4 cups thinly sliced or shredded
  green cabbage (about ½ head)
6 medium carrots, grated (about
  2 cups)
2 small yellow onions, halved and
  thinly sliced (about 1 cup)

In a small bowl, whisk together the mayonnaise, vinegar, and sugar. Season with a pinch of salt and twist of pepper. Add the cabbage, carrots, and onions and toss to combine. Let stand for 15 minutes before serving.

GRILLED SCALLOPS
+
CHARRED CAULIFLOWER STEAKS
+
GREMOLATA

Serves 4

One of the most memorable dishes I ever had was at chef Jean-Georges Vongerichten's first restaurant, JoJo, which opened in New York in 1991. Even though it was thirty years ago (geez, I'm old!), I still recall how those pan-roasted scallops tasted when paired with cauliflower, pine nuts, golden raisins, and brown butter. As a kid from the Midwest, the flavor profile of that dish was completely foreign to me but also very transformative. To this day, that experience shapes the way I think about food and cooking. Like that dish, this recipe is simple but elegant, with all the components working together in perfect harmony. Scallops and cauliflower might not sound like a typical pairing, but the sweetness from charring the vegetable on the grill really brings out the natural sweetness in the seafood. The gremolata adds the perfect counterpunch to the sweet, buttery scallops, which I grill instead of roast to get that essential crust. For this recipe, you'll want to char the cauliflower steaks on the hot side of the grill before moving them to the cooler side and putting the scallops on. Save the trimmed-off cauliflower pieces to make Cauliflower Puree (page 204).

12 sea scallops, side muscle removed
2 tablespoons extra-virgin olive oil
Kosher salt and freshly ground black pepper
Charred Cauliflower Steaks (page 106)
Gremolata (page 107)

1. Preheat a gas or charcoal grill for indirect cooking, with one hot side and one hold (unheated) side.

2. Pat the scallops dry with paper towels. Drizzle the scallops with the olive oil, tossing to coat evenly. Season the scallops on both sides with salt and pepper.

3. Place the scallops on the grill and cook, without moving, until nicely browned and they release from the grill, about 5 minutes. Use tongs to flip and continue cooking until the scallops are firm to the touch and cooked through, about 3 minutes.

4. Remove from the grill and serve with the cauliflower steaks and gremolata.

(recipe continues)

Charred Cauliflower Steaks

Serves 4

2 heads cauliflower
  (2 pounds each)
½ cup extra-virgin olive oil
1 teaspoon ground coriander
1 teaspoon ground cumin

Kosher salt and freshly ground
  black pepper
1 lemon, halved
Flaky sea salt

1. Remove the leaves and all but 1 inch of stem from the 2 heads of cauliflower. Working with one head at a time, place the head stem-side up on a cutting board. With a heavy, sharp knife, slice two 1-inch-thick "steaks" from the middle of the head. Repeat with the second head. Reserve the rest of the cauliflower (the rounded sides) for another use (such as adding to soup, salad, or processing into cauliflower "rice").

2. Preheat a gas or charcoal grill for indirect cooking, with one hot side and one hold (unheated) side.

3. In a small bowl, whisk together the olive oil, coriander, and cumin. Season with a pinch of kosher salt and twist of pepper.

4. Use a silicone brush to coat both sides of the cauliflower steaks with the spiced oil mixture.

5. Place the cauliflower steaks on the hot side of the grill and cook until nicely charred, about 5 minutes. Flip and cook until the second side is nicely charred, about 5 minutes. Move to the hold (unheated) side and cook until easily pierced by a fork, about 8 minutes.

6. Meanwhile, add the lemon halves cut-side down on the hot side of the grill and cook, without moving, for 5 minutes.

7. Transfer the cauliflower to a platter, squeeze the lemons over top, and sprinkle with sea salt.

Gremolata

Makes ½ cup

3 tablespoons extra-virgin olive oil
½ cup chopped fresh flat-leaf parsley

2 medium garlic cloves, minced
1 tablespoon grated lemon zest
1 teaspoon fresh lemon juice
¼ teaspoon kosher salt

In a medium bowl, stir together the olive oil, parsley, garlic, lemon zest, lemon juice, and salt. Let sit at room temperature for 30 minutes before serving. The gremolata can be refrigerated in an airtight container for up to 3 days.

GRILLED LOBSTER WITH LIME-JALAPEÑO BUTTER

+

SPICY OLD BAY CORN ON THE COB

Serves 4

When my longtime manager and friend Scott Feldman got married in Anguilla, Liz and I were fortunate to be able to make the trip. At the time, we were knee-deep in the restaurant world and the trip was our first big vacation in years. Near to where we were staying, there was a tiny shack selling grilled spiny lobsters that literally had just been pulled out of the water. They were basted with this amazing spicy butter sauce and I went back every single day that I was on the island. It was one of our favorite trips, and this dish always brings me right back to that sandy beach in Anguilla. In season, I eat as much sweet corn as humanly possible (maybe a little more, not gonna lie!). A secret to super-tender, super-flavorful grilled corn on the cob is to brine it first. Just pop the whole ears (after removing the silk, but not the husks) into salted water and let sit at room temperature for 1 to 2 hours.

2 sticks (8 ounces) unsalted butter, at room temperature
¼ cup finely chopped fresh cilantro
8 medium garlic cloves, grated
2 tablespoons minced jalapeño (with or without seeds)
Grated zest of 2 limes

Kosher salt and freshly ground black pepper
2 live lobsters (1½ to 2 pounds each)
2 tablespoons extra-virgin olive oil
Spicy Old Bay Corn on the Cob (page 110)

1. In a medium bowl, whisk together the softened butter, cilantro, garlic, jalapeño, and lime zest. Season with a pinch of salt and twist of black pepper.

2. Place one lobster belly-side up on a cutting board. Using a sharp chef's knife, spilt the lobster in half lengthwise, from head to tail. Repeat with second lobster. (Do this fast!) Scoop out and discard the soft green tomalley. Twist off the claws and crack them in a few places using the back of a chef's knife.

3. Preheat a gas or charcoal grill for indirect cooking, with one hot side and one hold (unheated) side.

4. Drizzle the cut (flesh) side of the lobsters with the olive oil and season with a few pinches of salt and twists of black pepper. Put the claws and lobsters cut-side down on the hot side of the grill and cook, without moving, until lightly charred, about 3 minutes. Flip and move the lobsters and claws to the hold side of the grill. Spread half the butter mixture evenly over the lobster meat and cook until the lobster is cooked through, about 4 minutes.

5. Serve the lobster and claws with remaining butter melted on the side for dipping and with the corn on the cob.

(recipe continues)

Spicy Old Bay Corn on the Cob

Serves 4

4 ears corn, unhusked
¼ cup kosher salt
⅓ cup mayonnaise (Duke's or
   Hellmann's)

1½ teaspoons Aleppo pepper
1 tablespoon Old Bay seasoning

1. Prepare the corn by peeling back the husks (don't remove them) to expose the silk. Remove as much of the silk as you can, then fold the husks back up over the corn.

2. In a large pot, combine 4 cups water and the salt and bring to a boil over high heat. Remove from the heat and stir in 8 cups cold water. Add the corn to the brine and let sit at room temperature for 1 to 2 hours.

3. Preheat a gas or charcoal grill for indirect cooking, with one hot side and one hold (unheated) side.

4. Remove the corn from the brine, allowing the excess water to drip off. Put all of the corn on the hold side of the grill, cover the grill, and cook for 10 minutes. Flip the ears and cook for 10 minutes.

5. Meanwhile, in a small bowl, mix together the mayonnaise, Aleppo pepper, and Old Bay.

6. When the corn is done, peel back the husks and liberally coat with the seasoned mayo.

GRILLED FLANK STEAK
+
FIRE-ROASTED POTATOES
+
BACON-ONION JAM

Serves 4

When I'm in the mood for skirt steak but can't seem to find it, flank steak makes a nice alternative. Both cuts take to the high heat of the grill well, both benefit from a well-seasoned marinade, and both have intensely beefy flavors. The big difference is that skirt is a little fattier, richer, and more tender. That's why I top this flank with a bacon and onion jam inspired by my buddy chef Josh Capon, who won Rachael's Burger Bash like seven times in a row. The potatoes are easy as can be because they are cooked in foil packets with lots of garlic, rosemary, and butter right on the hot coals in the grill. Just remember to start them well before the steak goes on. Also, as with skirt steak, flank steak should always be sliced against the grain. Any leftover bacon-onion jam can be stored in the fridge for up to 2 weeks.

1 (2-pound) flank steak
¼ cup plus 1 tablespoon extra-virgin olive oil
¼ cup packed light or dark brown sugar
2 tablespoons Worcestershire sauce
½ teaspoon sweet paprika
1 teaspoon Aleppo pepper
Kosher salt and freshly ground black pepper
Fire-Roasted Potatoes (page 114)
Bacon-Onion Jam (page 114)

1. Pierce the flank steak with a fork or paring knife a few times on both sides. Place the steak in a 1-gallon zip-top bag. In a small bowl, whisk together ¼ cup of the olive oil, the brown sugar, Worcestershire sauce, paprika, and Aleppo pepper. Season with a pinch of salt and twist of black pepper. Pour the marinade over the steak and refrigerate for up to 2 hours.

2. Preheat an outdoor grill to medium-high heat. Remove the steak from the refrigerator.

3. Remove the steak from the bag, allowing most of the marinade to drip off (discard the marinade). Pat the steak dry with paper towels. Drizzle the steak with the remaining 1 tablespoon olive oil and season both sides with salt and black pepper.

4. Put the steak on the grill and cook, without moving, until nicely charred, about 4 minutes. Flip and continue cooking until nicely charred and medium-rare, about 4 minutes.

5. Transfer the steak to a cutting board to rest, loosely tented with foil, for 5 minutes before slicing against the grain. Serve with the roasted potatoes and bacon jam.

(recipe continues)

Fire-Roasted Potatoes

Serves 4

4 large Yukon Gold potatoes, sliced into 1-inch-thick rounds
12 medium garlic cloves, unpeeled
4 sprigs fresh rosemary

4 tablespoons (½ stick) unsalted butter
Kosher salt and freshly ground black pepper
1 teaspoon Urfa pepper
1 cup chicken stock

1. Preheat a charcoal grill to high.

2. Cut off four 12 x 14-inch pieces of heavy-duty foil. In the center of each piece, put one-quarter of the potato slices, 3 whole garlic cloves, 1 sprig rosemary, and 1 tablespoon butter. Season each with a pinch of salt, a twist of black pepper, and ¼ teaspoon Urfa pepper. Lift all 4 corners of the foil up to begin to form a pouch. Before sealing, pour ¼ cup chicken stock into each packet. Tightly seal the seams of each packet. Fold the two longer edges of foil underneath each end to allow the potatoes to be propped up and not sitting directly on the coals.

3. When the coals are burning white, put the packets directly onto the hot coals (not on the grill grate). Cover the grill and cook until the potatoes are cooked through, about 45 minutes.

Bacon-Onion Jam

Makes 1¼ cups

1 tablespoon extra-virgin olive oil
½ pound sliced bacon, roughly chopped
3 large yellow onions, roughly chopped (about 3 cups)

Kosher salt
2 tablespoons sugar
¼ cup apple cider vinegar
Freshly ground black pepper

1. Line a plate with paper towels. Set a medium saucepan over medium-high heat. Add the olive oil and heat to shimmering, then add the bacon. Cook, stirring occasionally, until the bacon is crisp, about 8 minutes. Using a slotted spoon, transfer the bacon to the paper towels to drain.

2. Drain and discard (or save for another use) all but 2 tablespoons of the bacon fat. Set the saucepan over medium-low heat. Add the onions and a pinch of salt and cook, stirring occasionally, until deeply caramelized, about 20 minutes.

3. Add the sugar, stir, and continue cooking until the sugar dissolves, about 5 minutes. Add the vinegar, bring to a simmer, and cook until the sauce is reduced and jam-like, about 5 minutes. Remove from the heat, add the bacon, season lightly with salt and pepper, and stir to combine.

GRILLED SALMON STEAKS
+
GRILLED BOK CHOY
+
MUSTARD SAUCE

Serves 4

Salmon and swordfish are two of my favorite fishes to grill because they don't flake and fall apart like so many others. That means you can get a nice char on them before everything goes to pieces. If it's wild salmon season, by all means buy it if you can. Salmon and mustard go together like peas and carrots, and this velvety mustard cream sauce will make you weak in the knees. Try not to cook the salmon much past medium-rare because I feel that the flavor begins to change after that point (you can always tell it's done when it turns a deep red color and is just firm to the touch). Bok choy is loaded with vitamins, minerals, and antioxidants and cooking it quickly on the grill helps to preserve them. If you have an Asian market nearby, you'll be blown away by the incredibly varied selection of greens in addition to bok choy. Feel free to substitute any large, firm heads—like tatsoi, yu choy, or mustard greens—that look interesting.

4 skinless salmon steaks
 (8 to 10 ounces each)
⅓ cup extra-virgin olive oil
¼ cup reduced-sodium soy sauce
1 tablespoon Colman's English
 mustard

2 tablespoons finely chopped
 fresh cilantro
Kosher salt and freshly ground
 black pepper
Grilled Bok Choy (page 118)
Mustard Sauce (page 118)

1. Place the salmon in a 1-gallon zip-top bag.

2. In a large bowl, whisk together the olive oil, soy sauce, mustard, and cilantro. Reserve ⅓ cup marinade for basting and pour the remaining marinade over the salmon and refrigerate for 1 to 3 hours.

3. Preheat an outdoor grill or grill pan to medium-high heat.

4. Remove the salmon from the bag, allowing most of the marinade to drip off. Reserve the excess marinade for basting. Season both sides with salt and pepper. Put the fish on the grill and cook, without moving, until nicely browned and the fish releases from the grill, about 5 minutes. Flip and continue cooking, while basting the fish with the reserved marinade, for 3 minutes. Remove from the grill once the salmon is firm, deep red in color, and reaches an internal temperature of 145°F.

5. Serve with the bok choy and mustard sauce.

(recipe continues)

Grilled Bok Choy

Serves 4

2 large heads bok choy,
  quartered lengthwise
2 tablespoons extra-virgin
  olive oil

Kosher salt and freshly ground
  black pepper

1. Preheat an outdoor grill or grill pan to medium-high heat.

2. Drizzle the bok choy with the olive oil and season with a few pinches of salt and twists of black pepper. Put the bok choy on the grill and cook, without moving, until nicely browned on each side, about 3 minutes per side. Transfer to a platter and serve.

Mustard Sauce

Makes 1¼ cups

1 tablespoon extra-virgin olive oil
1 medium shallot, finely minced
  (about ¼ cup)
Kosher salt
½ cup dry white wine
1 tablespoon white wine vinegar
1 cup heavy cream

Freshly ground black pepper
1 tablespoon whole-grain
  mustard
2 teaspoons Dijon mustard
1 tablespoon thinly sliced fresh
  chives

1. Set a large saucepan over medium heat. Add the olive oil and heat to shimmering, then add the shallot and a pinch of salt. Cook, stirring occasionally, until the shallot softens, about 5 minutes.

2. Add the wine and vinegar, bring to a simmer, and cook until the liquid has almost completely evaporated, about 5 minutes. Add the cream, season with a pinch of salt and twist of pepper, and whisk to combine.

3. Bring the sauce to a boil (watch the pan closely so the cream doesn't boil over), then reduce the heat to medium-low to maintain a gentle simmer. Cook until the sauce has reduced and thickened, about 5 minutes. Remove from the heat, stir in both mustards and the chives, and serve.

GRILLED CHICKEN PAILLARD

+

CHARRED BROCCOLI RABE WITH GRILLED LEMONS

Serves 4

Typically, if I'm pounding out a piece of meat until it's wafer-thin, it's because I'm going to bread it and fry it like a schnitzel. Consider this a healthy schnitzel! After a quick soak in marinade to keep it flavorful and juicy, the flattened chicken breast cooks up in no time flat on the grill, in a grill pan, or, in a pinch, in a skillet. I love broccoli rabe so much, but sometimes the stems can be a little too thick and tough. A quick blanch, followed by an ice bath, solves that problem. Dry the vegetables well after the ice bath so they pick up a nice char from the grill. To serve, place the chicken on top of the rabe and squeeze the juicy grilled lemons over everything.

4 boneless, skinless chicken breasts (6 to 8 ounces each)
¼ cup extra-virgin olive oil
Grated zest and juice of 1 lemon
2 medium garlic cloves, grated
1 tablespoon finely chopped fresh rosemary
1 teaspoon Aleppo pepper
Kosher salt and freshly ground black pepper
Charred Broccoli Rabe with Grilled Lemons (opposite)

1. Place the chicken breasts on a large sheet of plastic wrap and cover with a second sheet. Use a meat mallet to pound the chicken to an even ¼-inch thickness. Place the chicken in a 1-gallon zip-top bag.

2. In a large bowl, whisk together the olive oil, lemon zest, lemon juice, garlic, rosemary, and Aleppo pepper. Season with a pinch of salt. Pour the marinade over the chicken and refrigerate for up to 2 hours.

3. Preheat an outdoor grill or grill pan to medium-high heat. Remove the chicken from the refrigerator.

4. Remove the chicken from the bag, allowing most of the marinade to drip off (discard the marinade). Season both sides of the chicken with salt and black pepper, place on the grill, and cook until nicely charred, about 4 minutes. Flip the chicken and continue cooking until the other side is also nicely charred and the chicken is fully cooked, about 3 minutes. Set aside to rest, loosely tented with foil, for 5 minutes before serving.

5. Plate the charred broccoli rabe and top with the chicken. Squeeze the grilled lemons over everything.

Charred Broccoli Rabe with Grilled Lemons

Serves 4

Kosher salt
2 pounds broccoli rabe, tough ends trimmed
4 tablespoons extra-virgin olive oil

Freshly ground black pepper
2 lemons, halved
½ teaspoon crushed red pepper flakes
Flaky sea salt

1. Set up an ice bath by filling a large bowl with ice and water.

2. Add 2 tablespoons kosher salt to a medium pot of water and bring to a boil over high heat. Add half of the broccoli rabe and cook until just al dente, about 1 minute. Use tongs to transfer the broccoli rabe to the ice bath. When cold, transfer the vegetables to a kitchen towel to dry, then place on a sheet pan. Add the remaining broccoli rabe to the boiling water and repeat the process.

3. Preheat an outdoor grill or grill pan to medium-high heat.

4. Drizzle the broccoli rabe with 2 tablespoons of the olive oil and season with a few pinches of kosher salt and twists of black pepper. Put the vegetables on the grill and cook, without moving, until nicely charred on both sides, about 2 minutes per side. Meanwhile, put the lemons on the grill cut-side down and cook, without moving, for 5 minutes.

5. Transfer the broccoli rabe to a platter, drizzle with the remaining 2 tablespoons olive oil, squeeze the lemons over top, and sprinkle with the pepper flakes and some flaky salt.

CRUNCHY FRIED CHICKEN

+

THROW-DOWN FRIED CHICKEN SAUCE

+

JOJO FRIES

Serves 4

I thought that my fried chicken was as good as it gets until chef Esther Choi took me to school on an episode of *Throwdown!* After tasting Choi's supremely crispy and flavorful Korean-style fried chicken, I knew that I had to up my game. The result is this recipe, which features an overnight brine to add flavor and moisture, and a double dredging in a combination of flour, rice flour, and cornstarch to construct the shell. To achieve that ultimate crunch, we fry the bird two separate times at two different temperatures, with an all-important rest period in between. What you end up with will absolutely blow your mind! If you've spent any time in the Akron and Kent areas of Ohio like I have, then you likely know and love jojos, chunky potato wedges with a crispy coating and creamy interior. After the chicken comes out of the oil the second time, wait for the oil to come back up to temp and drop the spuds. If you prefer a lighter side dish, I think either Cabbage and Carrot Slaw (page 102) or Charred Broccoli Rabe (page 123) would be great.

1 whole chicken (4 pounds), cut into 10 pieces
½ cup kosher salt
¼ cup packed light or dark brown sugar
1 jalapeño, quartered lengthwise
3 medium slices fresh ginger
3 medium garlic cloves, smashed

Neutral oil, for frying
2 cups all-purpose flour
1 cup rice flour
1 cup cornstarch
Throwdown Fried Chicken Sauce (page 127)
Jojo Fries (page 127)

1. Place the chicken in a large, sealable container.

2. In a large saucepan, bring 1 cup water to a simmer over medium-high heat. Add the salt and brown sugar and whisk until completely dissolved. Remove from the heat and add the jalapeño, ginger, garlic, and 3 cups cold water.

3. Pour the brine over the chicken, cover, and refrigerate overnight.

4. Pour 6 inches of neutral oil into a deep-fryer or deep heavy-bottomed pot and heat to 300°F. Set a wire rack over a sheet pan lined with paper towels.

(recipe continues)

5. Meanwhile, put the flour, rice flour, and cornstarch in a shallow bowl and whisk to combine. Working with 1 piece of chicken at a time, remove the chicken from the brine and dredge it in the flour mixture, making sure to coat all sides well. Shake off the excess. Dip the chicken back into the brine, allowing the excess to drip off. Return the chicken back to the flour mixture, turning and pressing to fully coat all sides. When done, arrange the chicken in an even layer on a wire rack while the oil heats.

6. Working in batches, if necessary, so as not to crowd the pan, fry the chicken until light golden brown and the meat reaches an internal temperature of 165°F, about 7 minutes. When done, use a slotted spoon or frying spider to transfer the chicken to the rack and let stand for up to 30 minutes while the oil heats to 360°F.

7. Working in batches again, if necessary, return the chicken to the pot and fry a second time until deep golden brown and crunchy, about 3 minutes. When done, transfer the chicken back to the rack and brush all sides with the throwdown sauce.

8. Serve with the jojo fries.

Throwdown Fried Chicken Sauce

Makes 1½ cups

1 cup plum wine
2 tablespoons grated fresh ginger
2 medium garlic cloves, grated
¼ cup soy sauce

1 tablespoon wasabi paste
8 tablespoons (1 stick) unsalted butter

In a medium saucepan, combine the plum wine, ginger, and garlic and bring to a strong simmer over medium-high heat. Cook until the liquid is reduced by half, about 6 minutes. Add the soy sauce and wasabi and bring to a boil. Remove from the heat and whisk in the butter until melted and smooth.

Jojo Fries

Serves 4

4 tablespoons (½ stick) unsalted butter, melted
½ cup all-purpose flour
1 teaspoon garlic powder
1 teaspoon sweet paprika

2 russet potatoes, cut lengthwise into quarters
Neutral oil, for frying
Kosher salt

1. Add the melted butter to a small bowl. In a 1-gallon zip-top bag, combine the flour, garlic powder, and paprika and shake to combine. Working with one potato wedge at a time, dip each wedge in the melted butter and then add it to the flour mixture. When all the wedges are in the bag, give them a shake to evenly coat. Arrange the wedges in an even layer on a wire rack while you preheat the oil.

2. Pour 6 inches of neutral oil into a deep-fryer or deep heavy-bottomed pot and heat to 360°F. Line a large plate with paper towels.

3. Working in batches so as not to crowd the pan, fry the potatoes until golden brown and crisp, using a slotted spoon or frying spider to turn them often, about 6 minutes. When done, remove the wedges using a slotted spoon and drain on the paper towels and season with salt immediately. Repeat with the remaining potatoes and serve while hot.

SHRIMP SCAMPI WITH LINGUINE + GREEN BEANS AND RADICCHIO

Serves 4

Shrimp scampi—which funnily enough translates to "shrimp shrimp"—is one of the most popular Italian American restaurant dishes. As a young chef working at an Italian restaurant, I always wanted guests to try my creative specials, but more often than not, they ordered the shrimp shrimp! Who can blame them? Shrimp sautéed in garlic butter and tossed in pasta is one of life's greatest joys! For this dish, try to find the biggest, freshest shrimp you can. The pasta is paired with a green bean and radicchio salad that is a riff on the classic green beans amandine.

Kosher salt
1 pound linguine
2 tablespoons extra-virgin olive oil
8 tablespoons (1 stick) unsalted butter
6 medium garlic cloves, thinly sliced
1 cup dry white wine
1 pound large shrimp, peeled and deveined
½ teaspoon crushed red pepper flakes
½ cup finely chopped fresh flat-leaf parsley
2 tablespoons fresh lemon juice
Green Beans and Radicchio (page 130)

1. Add 2 tablespoons salt to a large pot of water and bring to a boil over high heat. Add the pasta and cook, stirring occasionally so it doesn't stick together, for 2 minutes less than the package directions.

2. Meanwhile, set a large skillet over medium heat. Add the olive oil and 4 tablespoons of the butter and heat to shimmering, then add the garlic and a pinch of salt. Cook for 1 minute, then add the white wine and shrimp. Bring to a strong simmer and cook, stirring occasionally, until the wine has reduced slightly and the shrimp have cooked through, about 3 minutes. Add the pepper flakes, parsley, lemon juice, and remaining 4 tablespoons butter and stir until the butter has melted.

3. Reserving ½ cup of the pasta water, drain the pasta and transfer to the skillet. Add the reserved pasta water and toss to combine.

4. Serve with the green beans and radicchio on the side.

(recipe continues)

Green Beans and Radicchio

Serves 4

2 tablespoons red wine vinegar
2 teaspoons Dijon mustard
Kosher salt and freshly ground black pepper
¾ pound green beans, ends trimmed, cut into ½-inch lengths
¼ cup extra-virgin olive oil

1 small yellow onion, roughly chopped (about ½ cup)
2 medium garlic cloves, minced
½ cup sliced almonds
1 head radicchio, cored, quartered, and cut into 1-inch strips

1. In a small bowl, whisk together the vinegar and mustard. Season with a pinch of salt and twist of pepper. Set the vinaigrette aside.

2. Set up an ice bath by filling a large bowl with ice and water.

3. Add 2 tablespoons salt to a medium pot of water and bring to a boil over high heat. Add the green beans and cook until just al dente, about 2 minutes. Use a slotted spoon to transfer the beans to the ice bath. When cold, transfer the vegetables to a kitchen towel to dry.

4. Set a large skillet over medium heat. Add the olive oil and heat to shimmering, then add the onion and garlic. Season with a pinch of salt and twist of pepper. Cook, stirring occasionally, until the vegetables soften, about 5 minutes. Add the almonds and cook until the nuts are lightly toasted, about 3 minutes. Add the green beans, season with salt and pepper, and cook until the beans are warmed through, about 2 minutes.

5. In a large bowl, toss together the radicchio, green beans, and vinaigrette.

Turning Brisk

Throughout much of the country, autumn is one of the most magical times of the year. Mother Nature dials back the thermostat, lights up the trees with vividly colored leaves, and forces us to slow down thanks to shorter days. And according to people who actually sleep more than four hours a day, I hear it's a great season for that activity!

Fall is also when we celebrate my all-time favorite holiday, Thanksgiving, and foodwise there is so much to be thankful for. At the farmers' markets, home cooks say a bittersweet good-bye to tomatoes, peppers, corn, and cukes and a happy hello to apples, cabbage, Brussels sprouts, winter squashes, and root veggies, such as beets and sweet potatoes. Those ingredients form the backbone for increasingly heartier dishes like roasts, pasta bakes, and stews, which fill the house with the most intoxicating aromas. Will somebody please invent a Turkey and Sweet Potato Pie candle?!

Some of the recipes in this chapter require a little more preparation, cooking, and cleanup time, but I'd argue that the results are more than worth the effort.

Don't be afraid to substitute ingredients in or out based on personal preferences. Experiment with various winter squashes and root vegetables, swap one dried pasta for another, sample a new-to-you Asian green, and by all means go ahead and mix and match salads and sides from one main dish to another. There isn't just one right way to enjoy them!

PORK ROAST WITH CIDER-BRAISED ROOT VEGETABLES AND PAN GRAVY

Serves 6

This is a dish that my pap would make for the family on most New Year's Days and also for the occasional Sunday supper. I like to buy a pork rib roast and separate the ribs from the loin so that I can use the ribs as a sort of makeshift roasting rack for the loin—something I did with prime rib in my first cookbook, *Carnivore.* This allows each cut to cook to its appropriate temperature, ensuring that the pork loin and the pork ribs both come out perfect. The root veggies roast in those yummy pork juices in the roasting pan until everything is tender and then it all gets smothered in a cider-spiked pan gravy. Let me tell you how everybody fought over those pork ribs!

1 cup plus 1 tablespoon apple cider
2 tablespoons Dijon mustard
1 (6-rib) pork rack, bones removed and reserved
Kosher salt and freshly ground black pepper
2 tablespoons smoked paprika
2 carrots, cut into large cubes
2 parsnips, cut into large cubes
2 Yukon Gold potatoes, cut into large cubes
2 turnips, cut into large cubes
1 head garlic, separated into cloves, unpeeled
Small bunch of fresh thyme
1 tablespoon extra-virgin olive oil
2 tablespoons all-purpose flour
2 tablespoons finely chopped fresh flat-leaf parsley

1. Preheat the oven to 450°F.

2. In a small bowl, whisk together 1 tablespoon of the apple cider and the mustard. Coat all sides of the deboned pork rack with the mixture.

3. In a small bowl, stir together 1 tablespoon salt, 2 tablespoons black pepper, and the smoked paprika. Season all sides of the deboned pork rack and the reserved pork ribs with the paprika mixture. Put the ribs in a roasting pan bowed-side up. Set the deboned pork rack on top of the ribs so the ribs act as the roasting rack. Cook until the meat reaches an internal temperature of 145°F, about 30 minutes. Transfer the meat to a cutting board and loosely tent with foil. Leave the ribs in the roasting pan.

4. To the roasting pan, add the carrots, parsnips, potatoes, turnips, garlic, and thyme sprigs. Drizzle with the olive oil, season with salt and pepper, and return to the oven. Cook until the vegetables soften and the ribs reach an internal temperature of 195°F, about 30 minutes.

5. Transfer the ribs to a cutting board and loosely tent with foil. Transfer the vegetables to a platter.

6. Set the roasting pan over medium heat. Add the flour and cook, stirring, for 1 minute. While whisking, add 1 cup water and the remaining 1 cup apple cider and bring the sauce to a boil. Reduce the heat to medium-low to maintain a gentle simmer and cook, whisking occasionally, until the sauce thickens. Stir in the parsley.

7. Cut the ribs between the bones and add them to the platter of vegetables. Slice the meat and layer the pieces in an overlapping pattern on the platter. Spoon the pan gravy over the top and serve.

MARSALA AND MUSHROOM PASTA BAKE

+

SHAVED BRUSSELS SPROUT SALAD

Serves 4

This recipe is a riff on a dish of the same name that we made while filming *Symon's Dinners*. It resonated with viewers in a really big way, probably because it offers so much goodness in a single bite. You get the rich, savory, almost sherry-like undertones of a classic Marsala wine sauce, and you also get the supremely indulgent delights of a cheesy, baked-to-golden-brown-perfection pasta casserole. When it comes to the Marsala, I would say avoid the stuff at grocery stores sold as "cooking wine" if you can. You don't need to spend a ton of money for a bottle of drinkable Marsala, and the difference is night and day. And unlike regular wine, Marsala will last in your pantry for months after it's opened because of its higher alcohol content. I pair the pasta with an easy, but elegant, shaved Brussels sprout salad tossed with lots of grated pecorino cheese.

Kosher salt and freshly ground
  black pepper
1 pound cavatappi pasta
6 tablespoons unsalted butter
1 tablespoon extra-virgin olive oil,
  plus more as needed
1 yellow onion, thinly sliced
6 cups thinly sliced mixed
  mushrooms (shiitake and
  cremini)
2 medium garlic cloves, minced
1 tablespoon finely chopped fresh
  thyme
⅓ cup all-purpose flour

1 cup Marsala wine
3 cups vegetable broth
1 cup whole milk
Freshly grated nutmeg
½ cup finely chopped fresh
  flat-leaf parsley, plus more
  for serving
2 cups shredded low-moisture
  mozzarella cheese
Freshly grated parmesan cheese
  (finely grated on a Microplane),
  for serving
Shaved Brussels Sprout Salad
  (page 141)

1. Preheat the oven to 400°F.

2. Add 2 tablespoons salt to a medium pot of water and bring to a boil over high heat. Add the pasta and cook, stirring occasionally so it doesn't stick together, for 2 minutes less than the package directions. Drain the pasta.

3. In a large ovenproof skillet, heat the butter and olive oil over medium-high heat. When the butter has melted, add the onion and a pinch of salt. Cook, stirring occasionally, until the onion softens, about 5 minutes. Add the mushrooms and cook until golden brown and crisp, about 5 minutes. If the pan appears dry, add more olive oil. Add the garlic and thyme and cook for 1 minute. Add the flour and cook, stirring, for 1 minute. Whisking constantly, add the Marsala. Add the vegetable broth and milk and bring to a simmer. Season with a pinch of salt, a twist of pepper, and a dash of freshly grated nutmeg.

4. Add the drained pasta and parsley to the skillet and stir to combine. Top with the mozzarella, transfer to the oven, and bake until the cheese is golden brown and bubbling, about 10 minutes.

5. Top with parsley and parmesan and serve with the Brussels sprout salad.

(recipe continues)

Shaved Brussels Sprout Salad

Serves 4

½ cup pine nuts
¼ cup fresh lemon juice
2 teaspoons Dijon mustard
¼ cup extra-virgin olive oil
Kosher salt and freshly ground
    black pepper

1 scallion, white and light-green
    parts only, thinly sliced
4 cups shaved Brussels sprouts
    (about 1 pound)
⅓ cup finely grated pecorino
    cheese (about 1 ounce)

1. Preheat the oven to 350°F.

2. Arrange the pine nuts on a sheet pan and bake until lightly toasted, about 8 minutes.

3. In a medium bowl, whisk together the lemon juice and mustard. Whisking constantly, slowly add the olive oil. Season with a pinch of salt and twist of pepper. Add the scallion, Brussels sprouts, pecorino, and toasted pine nuts and toss to combine.

> Symon Says
>
> The mushroom sauce can be made up to 1 day ahead of time. You can also preheat the oven to 350°F in step 1 of the pasta bake recipe, toast the pine nuts, then increase the oven temperature to 400°F after they come out of the oven. When ready to serve, cook the pasta and toss with the warmed sauce before baking.

STOVETOP MAC AND CHEESE
+
BITTER GREENS SALAD

Serves 4 to 6

When it comes to macaroni and cheese, there are two types of cooks: those who bake it in the oven because it's hands-off easy and those who make it on the stovetop to keep it extra creamy. Personally, I land in the second camp, even though it might sadden my Southern relatives to hear me admit it. Too often, I feel, oven-baked mac and cheese winds up an overcooked, dry mess. By preparing it on the stovetop you're able to cook the pasta to the perfect texture while the dish retains its rich creaminess thanks to the silky cheddar and cream cheese sauce (cream cheese is the secret ingredient here). To get that nonnegotiable crispy top, we finish it with crunchy seasoned panko bread crumbs. And to counter all that over-the-top richness, I like to serve this with a bitter greens salad tossed in a honey-kissed vinaigrette.

4 cups shredded sharp cheddar
  cheese (about 1 pound),
  preferably yellow cheddar
1 tablespoon cornstarch
Kosher salt
1 pound cavatappi
4 cups heavy cream
8 ounces cream cheese

2 teaspoons Truff hot sauce (or
  your favorite hot sauce)
Freshly ground black pepper
3 tablespoons extra-virgin
  olive oil
1 cup panko bread crumbs
3 tablespoons thinly sliced fresh
  chives
Bitter Greens Salad (page 145)

1. In a large bowl, toss together the cheddar and cornstarch to fully coat. Set aside.

2. Add 2 tablespoons salt to a medium pot of water and bring to a boil over high heat. Add the pasta and cook, stirring occasionally so it doesn't stick together, for 2 minutes less than the package directions. Drain, rinse under cold water, and set aside.

3. In the same pot, bring the cream to a simmer over medium heat and cook until the liquid is reduced by one-third, about 12 minutes.

4. Add the cream cheese and whisk until it is melted and the sauce is smooth. Add the cheddar and whisk until smooth. Add the hot sauce, season with a few pinches of salt and twists of pepper, and stir to combine. Add the drained pasta, stir, and bring to a simmer. Remove from the heat and let stand, covered, for 5 minutes.

5. Meanwhile, set a large skillet over medium heat. Add the olive oil and heat to shimmering, then add the panko and stir to coat. Cook, stirring occasionally, until the panko is golden brown, about 5 minutes. Transfer to a bowl, season with a pinch of salt, and stir in the chives.

6. Spoon the macaroni and cheese into bowls, sprinkle with chive bread crumbs, and serve with the bitter greens salad.

(recipe continues)

Bitter Greens Salad

Serves 6

2 tablespoons red wine vinegar
1 tablespoon prepared
  horseradish
1 teaspoon Dijon mustard
½ teaspoon honey
⅓ cup extra-virgin olive oil
Kosher salt and freshly ground
  black pepper
2 heads Belgian endive, cored
  and separated into leaves

8 cups frisée, root ends removed,
  tops cut into 2-inch strips
  (8 cups after cutting)
2 cups sliced radicchio sliced
  ½-inch thick (from 1 to 2 cored
  and quartered heads)
½ cup fresh flat-leaf parsley
  leaves
½ cup 1-inch lengths fresh chives

1. In a small bowl, whisk together the vinegar, horseradish, mustard, honey, and olive oil. Season with a pinch of salt and twist of pepper.

2. In a large bowl, combine the endive, frisée, radicchio, parsley leaves, and chives. Add the dressing to taste, toss to combine, and garnish with more black pepper.

SWEET POTATO PIEROGIES + ROASTED KIELBASA WITH PICKLED MUSTARD SEEDS

Makes 24 pierogies

This dish has my pap's fingerprints all over it. It's still my go-to pierogi dough because it's so simple and easy to work with. Obviously, when it comes to fillings, the sky's the limit. In the fall, I like to use potatoes, sweet potatoes, or butternut squash. During summer, it's nice to keep things light with fresh veggies and cheese or even seafood. When paired with the smoky kielbasa and pickled mustard seeds (or Cleveland Caviar from Cleveland-based Old Brooklyn Mustards), this meal is what Cleveland dreams are made of. Keep in mind that this recipe makes more pierogies than you'll need for one meal. I figure, if you're going through the trouble of making them from scratch, you might as well make a big old batch. They freeze beautifully and last for up to 3 months in the freezer.

Dough

8 tablespoons (1 stick) unsalted butter, at room temperature
1 cup sour cream
1 large egg
1½ teaspoons kosher salt
2¼ cups all-purpose flour, plus more for rolling

Filling

2 large sweet potatoes (about 1 pound)
4 tablespoons (½ stick) unsalted butter
1 large shallot, finely chopped (about ½ cup)

Kosher salt
¼ cup roughly chopped fresh sage
½ cup mascarpone cheese
1 teaspoon freshly grated nutmeg
Freshly ground black pepper

Assembly and Serving

Kosher salt
4 tablespoons (½ stick) unsalted butter
¼ cup whole fresh sage leaves
Roasted Kielbasa with Pickled Mustard Seeds (page 149)
Pickled Mustard Seeds (page 149)

1. Make the dough: The day before, in a stand mixer fitted with the paddle, combine the butter, sour cream, egg, and salt. Add ¼ cup of the flour and mix on medium speed until blended and smooth. Switch to the dough hook, add the remaining 2 cups flour, and mix on medium speed until the dough pulls away from the bowl and begins to climb the hook, about 2 minutes. Turn the dough out onto a lightly floured surface and flatten it into a disc. Wrap in plastic and refrigerate overnight.

2. Make the filling (also the day before): Preheat the oven to 425°F. Line a sheet pan with foil.

3. Put the sweet potatoes on the prepared sheet pan and pierce them with a fork or paring knife a few times on all sides. Roast until very soft, about 1 hour. When cool enough to handle, scoop the flesh out into a food processor.

4. In a skillet, melt the butter over medium heat. Add the shallot and a pinch of salt and cook, stirring occasionally, until the shallot softens, about 3 minutes. Add the sage and cook for 1 minute. Transfer to the

(recipe continues)

food processor with the sweet potato. Add the mascarpone and nutmeg. Season with a pinch of salt and a twist of pepper. Process until smooth.

5. Place the sweet potato mixture in a cheesecloth-lined colander, set in a bowl, cover, and drain overnight in the refrigerator.

6. Assemble the pierogies: Line a sheet pan with parchment paper. Divide the dough into 2 equal portions. On a lightly floured surface, use a rolling pin to roll out one portion to a thickness of ¼ inch. Use a 3½- to 4-inch biscuit cutter to cut out dough rounds. Shake off any excess flour and transfer the rounds to the lined sheet pan. Repeat with the remaining portion of dough. Gather up the scraps, form into a smooth ball, and repeat the rolling and cutting process. You should end up with 24 rounds.

7. Dust a sheet pan with flour. Working with 6 rounds at a time, use a pastry brush to brush the surface of each dough round with water. Place 1 heaping tablespoon of filling in the center of the round. Fold and crimp the dough around the filling into a half-moon. Transfer the half-moon to the floured sheet pan. Repeat with the remaining dough and filling. Set aside 8 pierogies for serving. (The remainder can be refrigerated for up to 1 day or frozen for up to 3 months.)

8. Add 2 tablespoons salt to a large pot of water and bring to a boil over high heat. Add the 8 pierogies and cook until they float, about 5 minutes.

9. Meanwhile, in a large skillet, melt the butter over medium heat and cook, stirring, until the butter begins to brown and smell nutty, about 4 minutes. Add the sage and cook for 1 minute.

10. When the pierogies have floated to the top, use a slotted spoon to transfer them to the skillet. Add ¼ cup of the cooking water to the skillet and bring to a simmer. Flip the pierogies in the sauce to coat. Serve with the roasted kielbasa and the pickled mustard seeds.

Roasted Kielbasa with Pickled Mustard Seeds

Serves 4

2 pounds kielbasa
½ cup chicken stock or water

½ cup Pickled Mustard Seeds (below)

1. Preheat the oven to 400°F.

2. Line a sheet pan with heavy-duty foil. Set the kielbasa in the center and pierce it on the top with a fork or paring knife a few times. Bring up all 4 corners of the foil to begin to form a pouch. Pour in the stock and tightly crimp the foil. Place in the oven and bake until the sausage is golden brown and beginning to split, about 15 minutes.

3. Let rest for 5 minutes before slicing and serving with pickled mustard seeds.

Pickled Mustard Seeds

Makes 2 cups

1½ cups white wine vinegar
⅓ cup sugar

1 tablespoon kosher salt
¾ cup yellow mustard seeds

Set a medium saucepan over medium-high heat. Add the vinegar, sugar, salt, and ⅓ cup water and bring to a simmer, whisking to dissolve the sugar and salt. Add the mustard seeds and bring back to a simmer. Once the liquid is at a simmer, turn off the heat and set the pan aside, letting the mustard seeds cool in the liquid in the pan. Once cooled, transfer to an airtight container and refrigerate for up to 3 months.

CHICKEN AND PROSCIUTTO ROLLS

+ ROASTED ACORN SQUASH

+ SPINACH SALAD

Serves 4

This recipe is a twist on veal saltimbocca, the classic Roman dish of tenderized veal breast, prosciutto, and fresh sage. Here, I swap out the veal for more economical boneless chicken breasts, and I don't think the dish loses one bit of its appeal. As for the Marsala and Mushroom Pasta Bake (page 138), seeking out a better bottle of Marsala wine for this will make a big difference (and if you're buying it anyway, get good mileage out of it and make the pasta bake). In the fall, I roast a ton of acorn, delicata, and butternut squash—there's literally nothing easier, and few things are as delicious. To round out the meal, I make a big spinach salad with strawberries, goat cheese, and pistachios in a Champagne vinaigrette.

4 boneless, skinless chicken breasts (6 ounces each)
Kosher salt and freshly ground black pepper
16 fresh sage leaves
8 thin slices prosciutto
2 tablespoons extra-virgin olive oil

½ cup Marsala wine
¾ cup chicken stock
3 tablespoons unsalted butter
Roasted Acorn Squash (page 153)
Spinach Salad (page 153)

1. Place the chicken breasts on a large sheet of plastic wrap and cover with a second sheet. Use a meat mallet to pound the chicken to an even ¼-inch thickness. Season both sides of the chicken with salt and pepper.

2. Working with one piece of chicken at a time, arrange 4 sage leaves evenly across the surface. Top with 2 slices of prosciutto, overlapping if necessary. Starting on one end, roll the chicken into a tight cylinder, tucking the sides in as you go. Repeat with the remaining pieces of chicken, sage, and prosciutto. Wrap each piece tightly with plastic, twisting the ends, and refrigerate for at least 1 hour and up to overnight.

3. When ready to cook, unwrap the chicken and season on all sides with salt and pepper.

4. Set a large skillet over medium-high heat. Add the olive oil and heat to shimmering, then add the rolls, making sure to leave space between them. Cook, without moving, until the rolls are golden brown on all sides, about 8 minutes per side.

5. Drain any excess fat from the skillet and return the pan to medium-high heat. Add the Marsala and deglaze the pan, scraping with a wooden spoon around the rolls to loosen the browned bits on the bottom of the pan. Cook until the liquid has reduced by two-thirds, about 3 minutes. Add the chicken stock and bring to a simmer. Cook until the liquid has reduced slightly and the chicken is fully cooked, about 5 minutes. Transfer the chicken to a platter.

6. Whisk the butter into the Marsala sauce over medium-high heat until melted. Season with salt and pepper.

7. Spoon the sauce over the chicken rolls and serve with the squash and spinach salad on the side.

(recipe continues)

Roasted Acorn Squash

Serves 4

2 acorn squashes (1 to 1½ pounds each), quartered and seeded
2 tablespoons extra-virgin olive oil

Kosher salt and freshly ground black pepper
2 tablespoons honey

1. Preheat the oven to 400°F. Line a sheet pan with foil.

2. Place the squash skin-side down on the prepared sheet pan. Drizzle with the olive oil and season with a few pinches of salt and twists of black pepper.

3. Arrange the squash flesh-side down on the sheet pan and roast in the oven for 15 minutes. Flip the squash so that the other cut side is down and continue cooking for 15 minutes. Turn the squash so that it is skin-side down, baste with honey, and continue cooking until golden brown and very soft, about 15 minutes more.

Spinach Salad

Serves 4 to 6

¾ cup extra-virgin olive oil
¼ cup Champagne vinegar
1 tablespoon Dijon mustard
1 teaspoon honey
Kosher salt and freshly ground black pepper
12 ounces baby spinach leaves

1 small red onion, diced (about ½ cup)
2 cups quartered strawberries
4 ounces crumbled goat cheese (about ¾ cup)
½ cup chopped roasted, salted pistachios

1. In a small bowl, whisk together the olive oil, vinegar, mustard, and honey. Season with a pinch of salt and twist of pepper.

2. In a large bowl, combine the spinach and red onion. Add half the vinaigrette, season with salt and pepper, and toss to combine. Transfer to a serving bowl and top with the strawberries, goat cheese, and pistachios.

3. Any leftover dressing will hold in the refrigerator for up to 2 weeks.

TURKEY AND SWEET POTATO PIE
+
ROASTED RADICCHIO SALAD WITH PECANS

Growing up in the Midwest, raking leaves is practically a full-time job in autumn. Knowing that a pot pie like this was waiting for me on the other end of a chilly day outdoors was all the encouragement a kid could need. This hearty, comforting dish is loaded with ground turkey, bacon, sweet potatoes, and just a hint of cinnamon. The most difficult part of this recipe is making the dough, and even that's a breeze when you use a food processor. (Yes, you can use store-bought if you must, but please give homemade a try sometime!) The filling comes together in the time it takes for the dough to rest in the fridge, and while the pie is baking, you can move on to preparing the roasted radicchio salad. Roasting the typically bitter green tames the bite, brings out the sweetness, and makes it tender. It then gets tossed with dried cherries and pecans.

Serves 4 to 6

Pastry

3 cups all-purpose flour, plus more for rolling
1 teaspoon kosher salt
2 tablespoons sugar
2 sticks (8 ounces) unsalted butter, diced and chilled
6 to 8 tablespoons ice water

Filling

¼ pound thick-sliced bacon, diced
1 pound ground turkey (preferably a combo of light and dark meat)
Kosher salt and freshly ground black pepper

1 large sweet potato (about 8 ounces), peeled and medium diced
1 celery stalk, finely chopped (about ½ cup)
¼ cup roughly chopped celery leaves
2 large yellow onions, finely chopped (about 2 cups)
2 medium garlic cloves, minced
½ cup thinly sliced fresh flat-leaf parsley
⅛ teaspoon ground cinnamon
Egg wash: 1 egg yolk beaten with 1 tablespoon whole milk

Serving

Roasted Radicchio Salad with Pecans (page 157)

1. Make the pastry: In a food processor, combine the flour, salt, and sugar and pulse to combine. Add the butter and pulse until the mixture resembles small peas. With the machine running, gradually add ice water by the tablespoon until the dough just comes together in the bowl. You might not need to use it all. Turn the dough out onto a lightly floured surface and knead it into a cohesive ball. Divide the dough into 2 equal portions, flatten them into discs, wrap in plastic, and refrigerate for at least 30 minutes or up to overnight.

(recipe continues)

2. Make the filling: Line a plate with paper towels. In a large Dutch oven, cook the bacon over medium heat, stirring occasionally, until crisp, about 5 minutes. Using a slotted spoon, transfer to the paper towels to drain. Add the turkey to the Dutch oven and season with a pinch of salt and twist of pepper. Cook, stirring with a wooden spoon to break up the meat, until lightly browned, about 3 minutes. Use a slotted spoon to transfer to the plate with the bacon, leaving any remaining fat in the pan.

3. Add the sweet potato, celery, celery leaves, onions, and garlic to the Dutch oven and cook, stirring occasionally, until the vegetables begin to soften, about 5 minutes. Add 1 cup water to deglaze the pan, scraping with a wooden spoon to loosen the browned bits on the bottom. Stir in the parsley and cinnamon and return the bacon and turkey to the pot. Bring to a simmer and cook until the liquid has evaporated, about 20 minutes.

4. Preheat the oven to 400°F.

5. On a lightly floured surface, roll each dough disc into a 10-inch round. Carefully press one round into a 9-inch pie pan. Trim the dough to leave a 1-inch overhang all around. Pour the filling into the crust. Top with second dough round, trimming away any excess. Crimp the edges to seal.

6. Brush the top with the egg wash and season with a pinch of salt and twist of pepper. Using a sharp knife, cut a small slit into the center of the top crust to vent steam.

7. Bake until the crust is golden brown, about 45 minutes.

8. Let stand for 30 minutes before slicing. Serve with the radicchio salad.

Roasted Radicchio Salad with Pecans

Serves 4

½ cup pecans
2 heads radicchio, cored and quartered
2 tablespoons extra-virgin olive oil
2 tablespoons balsamic vinegar

Kosher salt and freshly ground black pepper
½ cup dried cherries, roughly chopped
¼ cup finely chopped fresh flat-leaf parsley
Flaky sea salt, for serving

1. Preheat the oven to 350°F.

2. Arrange the pecans on a sheet pan and cook until lightly toasted, about 8 minutes. Transfer to a bowl.

3. Increase the oven temperature to 425°F.

4. Arrange the radicchio quarters cut-side up on the sheet pan. Drizzle with the olive oil and vinegar and toss to coat. Season with a pinch of kosher salt and twist of pepper. Cook until the radicchio softens and browns around the edges, about 15 minutes.

5. Transfer to a platter and top with chopped cherries, parsley, and toasted pecans. Garnish with flaky sea salt and freshly ground black pepper.

MAPLE-GLAZED ROAST CHICKEN
+
BUTTERNUT SQUASH PUREE
+
ENDIVE AND APPLE SALAD

Serves 4

I will never, ever tire of roasting whole chickens. You get such bang for the buck when choosing whole over precut, there are a million and one variations you can try, and the leftovers are as good as the main meal. In fact, we often roast two whole chickens at a time just for that reason. For this recipe, the bird gets glazed in a sweet and savory maple and mustard glaze, which turns the skin a gorgeous chestnut brown. Inside the bird, orange slices, garlic, and sage flavor the meat while keeping it moist. I like to carve the meat and place it right on top of the butternut squash puree so the juices drip down into it. The tart apple and endive salad goes right on top of the chicken, adding that all-important zip and crunch.

¼ cup maple syrup
¼ cup Dijon mustard
¼ cup extra-virgin olive oil
1 whole chicken (about 4 pounds)
½ navel orange, halved
6 medium garlic cloves, peeled and whole

Small bunch of fresh sage
Kosher salt and freshly ground black pepper
Butternut Squash Puree (page 160)
Endive and Apple Salad (page 160)

1. Preheat the oven to 450°F. Line a sheet pan with foil.

2. In a medium bowl, whisk together the maple syrup, mustard, and olive oil.

3. Put the chicken breast-side up on the prepared sheet pan and tuck the wings behind the breasts. Put the orange halves, garlic cloves, and sage inside the cavity of the bird. Coat the exterior of the chicken with half the maple-mustard mixture and season with a few pinches of salt and twists of pepper.

4. Transfer to the oven and roast, basting the chicken with the glaze every 15 minutes, until the meat reaches an internal temperature of 165°F at the leg/thigh joint, about 1 hour.

5. Let rest for 15 minutes before carving. Serve the chicken with the squash puree and salad.

(recipe continues)

Turning Brisk

Butternut Squash Puree

Serves 4

1 (2-pound) butternut squash, halved lengthwise and seeded
2 tablespoons extra-virgin olive oil

Kosher salt and freshly ground black pepper
6 tablespoons unsalted butter
½ teaspoon freshly grated nutmeg

1. Preheat the oven to 400°F. Line a sheet pan with foil.

2. Arrange the squash skin-side down on the prepared sheet pan. Drizzle with the olive oil and season with a few pinches of salt and twists of black pepper. Flip the squash cut-side down and bake until very soft and golden brown, about 1 hour.

3. Meanwhile, in a medium saucepan, cook the butter over medium heat, stirring, until the butter begins to brown and smell nutty, about 5 minutes. Be careful not to let the butter burn. Remove from the heat.

4. While still warm, scoop out the flesh of the squash and transfer it to a blender. Add the brown butter and nutmeg. Season with a pinch of salt and twist of pepper and process until smooth.

Endive and Apple Salad

Serves 4

½ cup walnuts
3 tablespoons apple cider vinegar
1 tablespoon whole-grain mustard
¼ cup extra-virgin olive oil

Kosher salt and freshly ground black pepper
3 heads Belgian endive, cut into ½-inch lengths
2 tart medium apples, unpeeled, diced

1. Preheat the oven to 350°F.

2. Arrange the walnuts on a sheet pan and cook until lightly toasted, about 8 minutes. Transfer to a cutting board and when cool enough to handle, roughly chop.

3. In a medium bowl, whisk together the vinegar and mustard. Whisking constantly, slowly add the olive oil. Season with a pinch of salt and twist of pepper.

4. Add the endive, apples, and chopped walnuts to the dressing and toss to combine. Garnish with freshly ground black pepper.

CAST-IRON RIB EYES
+
CRISPY SMASHED POTATOES
+
FRISÉE AND BACON SALAD

Serves 4

Ask my neighbors: I'm the weirdo who fires up the grill in eight inches of freshly fallen snow. In Cleveland, we call that Tuesday. But even I have my limits and occasionally have to switch gears at the hands of Mother Nature. That's when I grab my trusty cast-iron skillet, blast the heat, and open all the kitchen windows to let out the smoke! A perfectly crusted steak from a screaming-hot cast-iron pan is *almost* as good as a well-charred steak from a wood-fired grill. If you don't have a large cast-iron griddle that can handle multiple steaks, you can use two separate skillets or cook the steaks in batches. To get the steakhouse-at-home vibe, I pair the chops with crispy smashed spuds and a bacon and frisée salad. Crack a bottle of red wine and call it a beautiful day!

4 rib-eye steaks, 2 inches thick
Kosher salt and freshly ground
   black pepper
2 tablespoons extra-virgin
   olive oil
2 tablespoons unsalted butter
4 medium garlic cloves, unpeeled
   and smashed

2 medium shallots, unpeeled and
   quartered
Small bunch of fresh oregano
1 lemon, halved
Crispy Smashed Potatoes
   (page 164)
Frisée and Bacon Salad
   (page 165)

1. Liberally season both sides of the steaks with salt and pepper.

2. Set a large cast-iron skillet over medium heat. Add the olive oil and heat to shimmering, then add the steaks. Cook until the first side is nicely charred, about 4 minutes. Flip and cook for 2 minutes. Add the butter, garlic, shallots, and oregano. When the butter has melted, carefully tilt the skillet and use a spoon to baste the steaks while they continue to cook for 2 minutes more. Squeeze both lemon halves into the pan and keep basting the steaks for another 2 minutes for medium-rare, longer if you prefer more doneness.

3. Loosely tent with foil and set aside to rest for 5 minutes before serving with the crispy potatoes and frisée salad.

(recipe continues)

Crispy Smashed Potatoes

Serves 4

2 tablespoons extra-virgin
  olive oil
2 pounds baby Yukon Gold or red
  potatoes
Kosher salt and freshly ground
  black pepper

4 medium garlic cloves, sliced
1 lemon, halved
2 tablespoons finely chopped
  fresh flat-leaf parsley
Flaky sea salt, for serving

1. Set a large heavy skillet over medium-high heat. Add 1 tablespoon of the olive oil and the potatoes, season with a pinch of kosher salt and twist of pepper, and add the garlic. Cook, shaking the pan occasionally, until the potatoes are golden brown on all sides, about 5 minutes.

2. Add enough water to come halfway up the sides of the potatoes. Cover and cook until the potatoes are tender, about 15 minutes. Drain any remaining liquid from the pan.

3. Using a potato masher or the back of a fork, lightly smash the potatoes to flatten them. Add the remaining 1 tablespoon olive oil and cook until the potatoes' bottoms are golden brown and crisp, about 3 minutes. Flip the potatoes and cook until the flipped side is also golden brown, about 3 minutes longer.

4. Squeeze the lemon halves over the potatoes, sprinkle with the parsley and flaky salt, and serve.

Frisée and Bacon Salad

Serves 4

4 large eggs
¼ cup plus 1 tablespoon extra-virgin olive oil
½ pound bacon, chopped
3 tablespoons Champagne vinegar
2 teaspoons Dijon mustard
Kosher salt and freshly ground black pepper
2 heads frisée, root ends trimmed off, cut into 2-inch pieces (about 4 cups)
½ cup fresh flat-leaf parsley leaves

1. Bring a medium pot of water to a boil over high heat. Reduce the heat to medium-low to maintain a gentle simmer, carefully add the eggs, and cook, uncovered, for 15 minutes.

2. Meanwhile, set up an ice bath by filling a large bowl with ice and water.

3. When the eggs are done, transfer them to the ice bath to cool for 5 minutes. Drain, peel, and quarter the eggs.

4. Line a plate with paper towels. Set a large skillet over medium-high heat. Add 1 tablespoon of the olive oil and heat to shimmering, then add the bacon and cook, stirring occasionally, until golden brown and crispy, about 5 minutes. Transfer to the paper towels to drain.

5. In a medium bowl, combine the vinegar and mustard. Whisking constantly, slowly add the remaining ¼ cup olive oil in a steady stream. Season with a pinch of salt and a twist of pepper. Add the frisée and parsley and toss to coat.

6. Transfer the salad to a platter, top with the quartered eggs, and garnish with the bacon and freshly ground black pepper.

SHELLS WITH CLAMS + CLASSIC CAESAR SALAD

Serves 4

Oh man, does this recipe scream classic Italian dinner. There is no shortage of linguine with clams recipes out there, but this one goes the extra mile to capture the true essence of the dish. In place of canned clams and bottled clam juice, we use two types of live clams and make our own flavorful broth. It's easier than it sounds! That broth turns into the most amazing clam sauce for the pasta. It has never been easier to find pancetta, which is like bacon but without all that smokiness. The meat lends such a pleasant brininess—as do the clams—that we don't even add any salt when cooking. For my fellow Cleveland Browns fans out there, this dish is the Bernie Kosar of dinners: consistent but never flashy, and always brings a smile to your face. Store any leftover Caesar dressing in the refrigerator up to 1 week.

1¼ cups dry white wine, plus more if needed
2 dozen cherrystone clams, scrubbed and cleaned
½ cup extra-virgin olive oil
¼ pound pancetta, finely chopped
2 celery stalks, finely chopped (about 1 cup)
3 medium shallots, finely chopped (about ¾ cup)

4 medium garlic cloves, thinly sliced
Pinch of crushed red pepper flakes
½ cup thinly sliced fresh flat-leaf parsley, plus more for serving
Kosher salt
1 pound medium pasta shells
1 dozen littleneck clams
Classic Caesar Salad (page 169)

1. Set a large Dutch oven over high heat. When the pan is hot, add 1 cup of the wine and the cherrystone clams. Cover and cook for 5 minutes. Uncover and, using tongs, begin transferring the open clams to a large bowl. If some clams still haven't opened, cover and cook for another 45 seconds before checking again. Discard any clams that still have not opened.

2. Line a fine-mesh sieve with a double layer of cheesecloth and set over a bowl. Strain the clam broth in the Dutch oven (and any juices that might have accumulated in the large bowl of cooked clams) through the sieve. Strain the broth a second time through a fresh double layer of cheesecloth to remove all grit. You should end up with about 2 cups of liquid. If not, top off with water or white wine.

3. When the clams are cool enough to handle, remove them from their shells, then discard the shells. To prepare the clams, remove and discard the abductor muscle. Cut the clams in half and clean out the digestive tract. Roughly chop the clams.

(recipe continues)

4. Wipe out the Dutch oven and set over medium heat. Add the olive oil and heat to shimmering, then add the pancetta. Cook, stirring occasionally, until the pancetta is very crisp, about 5 minutes. Add the celery, shallots, and garlic and cook, stirring occasionally, until the vegetables soften, about 10 minutes. Add the strained clam broth and pepper flakes and bring to a simmer. Remove from the heat and add the chopped clams and parsley. Keep warm over very low heat.

5. Add 2 tablespoons salt to a large pot of water and bring to a boil over high heat. Add the pasta and cook, stirring occasionally so it doesn't stick together, for 1 minute less than the package directions.

6. Meanwhile, set a large skillet over high heat. When the pan is hot, add the remaining ¼ cup wine and the littleneck clams. Cover tightly and cook until the clams have opened, about 2 to 4 minutes. Discard any unopened clams.

7. Drain the pasta and add it to the clam sauce. Sprinkle in more parsley and stir to combine. Transfer to a large platter, arrange the littleneck clams around the pasta (discarding any accumulated juices in the skillet), and serve with the Caesar salad.

Symon Says

You can refrigerate the clam sauce for up to a day before serving. Warm the clam sauce in a saucepan while the pasta cooks and proceed with the recipe.

Make the Caesar dressing (refrigerate in an airtight container) and croutons (store in an airtight container) up to 1 day ahead of time.

Classic Caesar Salad

Serves 4

4 cups large-diced ciabatta bread
½ cup plus 3 tablespoons extra-virgin olive oil
Kosher salt and freshly ground pepper
1 large garlic clove, peeled
3 white anchovy fillets
2 large egg yolks
1 teaspoon Worcestershire sauce
1 teaspoon Dijon mustard

Juice of 2 lemons
¼ cup freshly grated parmesan cheese (finely grated on a Microplane)
3 romaine hearts, cored and separated into leaves
Shaved parmesan cheese, for serving
Whole white anchovies, for serving

1. Preheat the oven to 350°F.

2. In a large mixing bowl, add the diced bread, drizzle with 3 tablespoons of the olive oil, and toss to combine. Season with a pinch of salt and twist of pepper. Arrange the bread cubes on a sheet pan and bake, stirring halfway, until golden brown, about 15 minutes.

3. Spear the garlic clove onto the tines of a fork and rub it all over the inside of a salad bowl. Discard any remaining garlic or save for another use.

4. To the same bowl, add the 3 anchovies and ½ teaspoon salt and mash them with the back of a fork to a fine paste. Add the egg yolks, Worcestershire, mustard, lemon juice, and the remaining ½ cup olive oil and mix vigorously with a fork. Add the grated parmesan and 10 turns of black pepper and stir to blend. Add the romaine leaves and toss gently to evenly coat.

5. Divide the lettuce onto four plates and garnish with the croutons, shaved parmesan, and whole anchovies.

BRACIOLE
+
PARMESAN POLENTA
+
POMODORO SAUCE

Serves 4 to 6

No surprise, many of my fondest memories from childhood involve food. Growing up, food and family were inseparable concepts in my mind. To this day, when I think of my grandmother on my mom's side, I can practically smell and taste her incredible braciole and soft polenta. She'd often make it for us on long, lazy Sundays—the whole house would be perfumed with the sweet smell of meat simmering in tomato sauce. Hot damn, now I'm hungry! The genius of this dish is that it uses an inexpensive cut of beef, which is pounded and then braised until tender in the sauce. Meanwhile, the beef lends its flavor to the sauce. Served on top of creamy soft polenta and topped with sauce, there is nothing better. If you're crunched for time, you can swap a 28-ounce can of good-quality crushed tomatoes for the homemade pomodoro. It will still be amazing. But if you do decide to make this super-simple four-ingredient pomodoro sauce, consider making a double batch to freeze half for an easy midwinter, midweek pasta feast.

½ cup pine nuts
½ cup golden raisins
½ cup dry Marsala wine
4 tablespoons extra-virgin olive oil
1 cup chopped fresh flat-leaf parsley
3 medium garlic cloves, minced
½ cup finely grated parmesan cheese (about 1½ ounces)
Grated zest of 1 orange
4 chuck shoulder steaks (10 ounces each)

24 very thin slices soppressata (about ½ pound)
2⅔ cups shredded fontina cheese (about ¾ pound)
Kosher salt and freshly ground black pepper
1½ cups dry red wine
3 cups Pomodoro Sauce (page 174) or store-bought crushed tomatoes
1½ cups chicken stock
Parmesan Polenta (page 174)

1. Preheat the oven to 350°F.

2. Arrange the pine nuts on a sheet pan and cook until lightly toasted, about 8 minutes. Set aside. Leave the oven on, but reduce the oven temperature to 325°F.

3. In a small saucepan, combine the raisins and Marsala and bring to a simmer over medium-high heat. Remove from the heat and let stand for 5 minutes to rehydrate.

4. In a medium bowl, combine 2 tablespoons of the olive oil, ½ cup of the parsley, the garlic, parmesan, orange zest, and Marsala-soaked raisins (and any remaining liquid) and stir to combine. Set aside.

5. Working with one steak at a time, place the meat on a large sheet of plastic wrap and cover with a second sheet. Use a meat mallet to pound the meat to an even ⅛-inch thickness. Repeat with the other steaks. Cut the steaks into long strips about 3 to 4 inches wide and 11 to 12 inches long. You will end up with 8 strips of meat.

6. Set a strip of meat with a long side facing you. Spread 2 tablespoons of the filling the length of the beef. Top with 3 pieces of overlapping soppressata, followed by ⅓ cup of the fontina. Starting at a short side, roll the beef into a tight cylinder and secure with toothpicks. Repeat with the remaining pieces of beef, filling, soppressata, and fontina.

7. Season all sides of the braciole with salt and pepper. Set a large heavy ovenproof skillet over medium-high heat. Add the remaining 2 tablespoons olive oil and heat to shimmering, then add the braciole, making sure to leave space between them. Cook, without moving, until golden brown on all sides, about 2 minutes per side. Add the red wine and deglaze the pan, scraping with a wooden spoon to loosen the browned bits on the bottom of the pan. Add the pomodoro and chicken stock and bring to a strong simmer.

8. Transfer the skillet to the oven and cook, uncovered, for 1½ hours, basting the meat every 20 minutes and flipping the pieces after 45 minutes.

9. Let rest for 15 minutes before garnishing with the remaining ½ cup parsley. Serve with braising sauce and the parmesan polenta.

(recipe continues)

Parmesan Polenta

Serves 4

¼ cup extra-virgin olive oil
2 teaspoons kosher salt
1½ cups quick-cooking polenta or fine cornmeal

½ cup finely grated parmesan cheese (about 1½ ounces)

In a medium saucepan, combine the olive oil, salt, and 6 cups water and bring to a boil over medium-high heat. Whisking constantly, slowly add the polenta. Reduce the heat to low and cook, stirring occasionally, until thick and smooth, about 10 minutes. Remove from the heat and stir in the parmesan.

Pomodoro Sauce

Makes 3 cups

6 tablespoons unsalted butter
1 (28-ounce) can whole peeled tomatoes

1 small yellow onion, peeled and quartered
Kosher salt and freshly ground black pepper

1. In a large saucepan, combine the butter, tomatoes, onion, a pinch of salt, and a twist of pepper. Bring the sauce to a boil over medium-high heat. Reduce the heat to medium-low to maintain a gentle simmer and cook, stirring occasionally, for 45 minutes.

2. Remove from the heat, carefully transfer to a blender or food processor, and process until smooth. Use immediately or store for 5 days in the refrigerator or freeze for up to 1 month.

SEAFOOD STEW

\+

SAFFRON AIOLI

\+

GRILLED BREAD

Serves 4 to 6

I spend a lot of time on Long Island these days, close to our son, Kyle, and our grandkids. While there are a million reasons to love the location, it's the seasonal produce and pristine seafood that really puts it over the top for me. We're surrounded by amazing farmers' markets and shops selling the freshest possible fish. This recipe is such a simple but stunning way to cook mussels, shrimp, and halibut. As it cooks, the seafood flavors the sauce and the sauce keeps the fish from drying out. I know saffron isn't cheap, but trust me when I tell you that the saffron aioli sends this dish into the stratosphere. And you absolutely have to have plenty of crusty grilled bread for mopping up every last drop of the dreamy seafood broth! Any leftover aioli would go great with foods like roasted potatoes, fried fish, or peel-and-eat shrimp.

1 tablespoon extra-virgin olive oil
2 large yellow onions, finely chopped (about 2 cups)
3 medium garlic cloves, thinly sliced
Kosher salt
½ teaspoon crushed red pepper flakes
1 dozen littleneck clams, scrubbed
½ cup Pernod
1 cup dry white wine

1 (28-ounce) can tomato puree
Freshly ground black pepper
2 dozen mussels, scrubbed
½ pound large shrimp, peeled and deveined
1 pound skinless halibut
¼ cup roughly chopped fresh tarragon
¼ cup thinly sliced fresh chives
Flaky sea salt, for serving
Grilled Bread (page 178)
Saffron Aioli (page 178)

1. Set a large Dutch oven over medium heat. Add the olive oil and heat to shimmering, then add the onions, garlic, and a pinch of kosher salt. Cook, stirring occasionally, until the vegetables soften, about 3 minutes. Add the pepper flakes and clams and stir to combine. Cover and cook for 2 minutes. Add the Pernod and cook until reduced by half, about 1 minute. Add the wine and tomato puree and bring to a strong simmer. Season with a pinch of kosher salt and twist of black pepper.

2. Add the mussels and stir to combine. Add the shrimp and stir to combine. Lay the halibut on top of the shellfish, cover, and cook until the clams and mussels have opened and the halibut is almost cooked through, about 3 minutes. Remove from the heat and let stand, covered, for 5 minutes.

3. Gently split the halibut into large pieces, stir in the tarragon and chives, and garnish with flaky salt. Serve with grilled bread and aioli.

(recipe continues)

Saffron Aioli

Makes 1 cup

2 tablespoons fresh lemon juice
¼ teaspoon saffron threads
2 large egg yolks
2 teaspoons Dijon mustard

1 medium garlic clove, grated
Kosher salt
¾ cup canola oil
¼ cup extra-virgin olive oil

1. In a small bowl, whisk together the lemon juice and saffron and let stand for 15 minutes.

2. In a blender or food processor, combine the egg yolks, mustard, garlic, and saffron mixture. Season with a pinch of salt. With the machine running, slowly add the oils one at a time in a steady stream and process until smooth. Refrigerate until needed.

Grilled Bread

Serves 6

6 slices (1 inch thick) rustic bread
3 tablespoons extra-virgin
   olive oil

Kosher salt and freshly ground
   black pepper

1. Preheat an outdoor grill or grill pan to medium-high heat.

2. Drizzle both sides of the bread with olive oil and season with a few pinches of salt and twists of pepper. Put the bread on the grill and cook until nicely charred, about 30 seconds per side.

PAN-ROASTED DUCK WITH ORANGE SAUCE AND PARSLEY SALAD

Serves 4

You don't see duck à l'orange on many restaurant menus these days, but when I was a young chef, it was still very popular. You could base an entire cooking class around mastering just this one dish. This is definitely not a "Five in Five" recipe, but for duck lovers, the payoff is more than worth the extra effort—and sometimes, a little bit of a project meal is just the thing on a rainy weekend day. Most of the time, when you order duck breast in a restaurant, it is served between rare and medium-rare. I prefer to push mine to medium—and maybe a hair (make that a feather) past—with cracker-crisp skin, of course. The brightness of the parsley salad, while not traditional, helps cut through the richness of the meat and sauce.

Fortified Stock

4 cups chicken stock
1 cup dry red wine
2 small yellow onions, roughly chopped (about 1 cup)
1 medium carrot, roughly chopped (about ½ cup)
1 celery stalk, roughly chopped (about ½ cup)
2 lemongrass stalks, bruised and cut into 3-inch pieces
2 medium garlic cloves
2 fresh bay leaves
1 small bundle of fresh thyme
Kosher salt

Cider-Citrus Gastrique

⅓ cup apple cider vinegar
⅓ cup sugar
1 cup freshly squeezed orange juice

Duck

4 Moulard duck breasts
Kosher salt and freshly ground black pepper
1 tablespoon extra-virgin olive oil
2 whole star anise
2-inch piece fresh ginger, sliced
1 small bundle of fresh thyme

Parsley Salad

1 cup fresh flat-leaf parsley leaves
½ cup orange supremes
Extra-virgin olive oil, for drizzling
Kosher salt

Finishing

2 tablespoons Grand Marnier
2 tablespoons cold unsalted butter
1 tablespoon thinly sliced fresh flat-leaf parsley
Freshly ground black pepper

1. Make the fortified stock: In a large saucepan, combine the chicken stock, wine, onions, carrot, celery, lemongrass, garlic, bay leaves, thyme, and a large pinch of salt. Bring to a boil over medium-high heat. Reduce the heat to medium-low to maintain a gentle simmer and cook, stirring occasionally, for 1 hour.

2. Make the cider-citrus gastrique: When the fortified stock is almost ready, in a medium saucepan, combine the vinegar and sugar and bring to a simmer over medium heat, whisking to dissolve the sugar. Add the orange juice and cook until reduced to a thick syrup, about 25 minutes. (You should end up with ½ cup.)

(recipe continues)

3. Strain the fortified stock through a fine-mesh sieve and discard the solids. Add ½ cup of the strained stock to the gastrique. (The remaining fortified stock can be refrigerated for up to 1 week or frozen for up to 1 month for another use.) Cook until the gastrique is reduced by half, about 10 minutes. Reduce the heat to low.

4. Prepare the duck: Using a very sharp knife, make a crosshatch pattern into the skin of the duck breasts, being careful not to cut into the meat. Season both sides of the meat with salt and pepper. Add the olive oil to a cold large skillet and add the breasts skin-side down. Set the skillet over medium-low heat and cook until much of the fat has rendered and the skin is golden brown and crisp, about 10 minutes. Flip and cook for 1 minute, then add the star anise, ginger, and thyme. Carefully tilt the skillet and use a spoon to baste the duck while it continues to cook for 5 minutes. Transfer the duck to a cutting board and loosely tent with foil. (Reserve the skillet.)

5. Make the parsley salad: In a medium bowl, combine the parsley leaves, orange supremes, and their juices. Drizzle with olive oil, season with a pinch of salt, and toss to combine.

6. To finish: Drain off any excess fat from the skillet and set over medium heat. Carefully add the Grand Marnier and, if using a gas burner, tilt the pan to ignite the alcohol. If electric, use a lighter. When the flames die out, add the reserved orange sauce and cook until warmed through. Add the cold butter and sliced parsley, season with a twist of black pepper, and stir to combine.

7. Thinly slice the breast against the grain. Arrange the duck slices skin-side up on a platter, drizzle with the sauce from the skillet, top with the parsley salad, and serve.

Symon Says

Make the fortified stock up to 2 days ahead of time and keep it chilled. Warm over medium-low when you're ready to finish the dish. (Wait to flambe until just before serving.)

BAKED ZITI
+
ESCAROLE WITH ANCHOVY-GARLIC BREAD CRUMBS

Serves 4

This recipe is proof that food doesn't have to be fancy or complicated to be amazing. I've been enjoying baked ziti—and variations of it—since I was old enough to eat solid foods, and it still rocks my socks! The key to recipes like these, ones with so few moving parts, is to use the best-quality ingredients possible. Homemade Pomodoro Sauce (page 174), low-moisture mozzarella, and genuine Parmigiano-Reggiano transform this meal from a great one to an award-winner. Even if you think you don't like anchovies, you should give the grilled escarole salad a try just to taste the anchovy-garlic bread crumbs. The salty-crunchy topping is so delicious that you'll be adding it to everything from pastas to grilled fish for that umami oomph.

Kosher salt
1 pound ziti
3 cups Pomodoro Sauce (page 174) or store-bought marinara
½ cup freshly grated parmesan cheese (finely grated on a Microplane)

2 cups shredded low-moisture mozzarella cheese
¼ cup thinly sliced fresh basil leaves
Escarole with Anchovy-Garlic Bread Crumbs (page 186)

1. Preheat the oven to 350°F.

2. Add 2 tablespoons salt to a medium pot of water and bring to a boil over high heat. Add the ziti and cook, stirring occasionally so it doesn't stick together, for 2 minutes less than the package directions. Drain the pasta and rinse.

3. Set a shallow Dutch oven over medium heat and add the pomodoro sauce. Add the ziti, stir to combine, and remove from the heat. Stir in ¼ cup of the parmesan and top with the mozzarella.

4. Transfer to the oven and bake, uncovered, until golden brown and bubbling, about 20 minutes. Remove from the oven and top with the remaining ¼ cup parmesan.

5. Let stand for 5 minutes before garnishing with basil and serving with the escarole.

(recipe continues)

Escarole with Anchovy-Garlic Bread Crumbs

Serves 4

Vinaigrette

4 white anchovy fillets, finely chopped
3 tablespoons white wine vinegar
2 teaspoons Dijon mustard
2 medium garlic cloves, minced
½ cup extra-virgin olive oil
Kosher salt and freshly ground black pepper
1 scallion, thinly sliced
1 tablespoon thinly sliced fresh chives

Bread Crumbs

3 cups diced ciabatta bread (about ¼ of a large loaf)
¼ cup extra-virgin olive oil
2 medium garlic cloves, grated
2 large white anchovies, minced

Assembly

2 heads escarole, outer leaves removed, halved lengthwise
2 tablespoons extra-virgin olive oil
Kosher salt and freshly ground black pepper
½ cup fresh flat-leaf parsley leaves

1. Make the vinaigrette: In a medium bowl, combine the anchovies, vinegar, mustard, and garlic. Whisking constantly, slowly add the olive oil in a steady stream. Season with a pinch of salt and a twist of pepper. Add the scallions and chives and stir to combine.

2. Make the bread crumbs: In a food processor, pulse the bread until it has the consistency of coarse crumbs (larger than panko but smaller than a crouton). Set a large skillet over low heat. Add the olive oil, garlic, and anchovies and cook, stirring occasionally, until the garlic is aromatic and the anchovies have broken down, about 2 minutes. Add the bread crumbs and stir to coat. Increase the heat to medium and cook, stirring occasionally, until the bread is golden brown, about 8 minutes.

3. To assemble: Preheat an outdoor grill or grill pan to medium-high heat.

4. Drizzle the escarole with the olive oil and season with a few pinches of salt and twists of black pepper. Put the escarole cut-side down on the grill and cook, without moving, until nicely charred, about 2 minutes. Flip and continue cooking for 1 minute. Transfer to a cutting board and when cool enough to handle, cut into 2-inch pieces.

5. In a large bowl, combine the grilled escarole and parsley leaves. Dress the salad to taste with the vinaigrette and toss to combine. Transfer to a platter and top with the anchovy bread crumbs. Any leftover vinaigrette will keep refrigerated for 2 weeks.

Cozy Comfort

The recipes in this chapter are some of the most personal ones in the entire cookbook. Along with those in the Holidays chapter (page 244), these meals are a true expression of my childhood growing up in Cleveland. This is stick-to-your-ribs comfort food, often with heavy Eastern European roots given the city's robust immigrant population. While recipes like Stuffed Cabbage in Tomato Sauce (page 221), Chicken Paprikash (page 207), and Beef Stew (page 225) sound tailor-made for a midwinter Midwestern meal, our family enjoyed them throughout the year. On any given Sunday, it was the Ricotta Cavatelli (page 194) that likely landed on the dinner table. Classic Meatloaf (page 212) and stuffed cabbage were often midweek staples all year long. If you were wondering where my "petite" physique originated, now you know!

Most of these recipes are front-loaded, meaning there's a bit of work to do at the start — like Beef Stew, Stuffed Cabbage, and Sunday Sauce — but once you get past that part, they are pretty much hands-off for the rest of the cooking period. Occasionally, you'll probably want to stroll by, give the dish a stir, and dunk a piece of bread in there to make sure it tastes as delicious as it smells. When the main course is almost ready, you can whip together the accompanying salad and/or side and serve it all family-style. If you love leftovers as much as I do, then this chapter is for you. Many of the dishes that follow somehow get better the following day or even the day after that, especially when enjoyed by a crackling fire watching your beloved football team break your heart. In Cleveland, that's called Sunday.

SUNDAY SAUCE
+
RICOTTA CAVATELLI
+
MOM'S SALAD

Serves 4 to 6

Growing up, the "heart" of our house on Sundays was the large pot of sauce that slowly burbled away on the stovetop. I can still recall the maneuvers I would attempt just to sneak into the kitchen so I could dunk bread into the pot to steal a taste. Loaded with flavorful meats like beef shin, veal shin, and sausage, the sauce—or gravy, as other families called it—takes on an incredible flavor. When paired with homemade cavatelli (a delicate ricotta-enriched pasta that we'd roll together on a floured wooden table), that sauce becomes the basis for the King of Sunday Suppers. To round out this feast, my mom would make her classic Sunday salad loaded with crisp romaine, tomatoes, and cucumbers. This sauce will still be amazing if you skip making the meatballs. Also, the meatballs are just as delicious on their own!

Sunday Sauce

3 tablespoons extra-virgin olive oil
3 pounds beef shin
3 pounds veal shin
Kosher salt and freshly ground black pepper
1 pound spicy Italian pork sausage links, casings removed
1 large onion, finely chopped
3 medium garlic cloves, thinly sliced
2 (28-ounce) cans crushed San Marzano tomatoes, undrained

Serving

Ricotta Cavatelli (page 194), cooked and drained
Freshly grated parmesan cheese
Torn fresh basil leaves
Mom's Salad (page 194)

1. Set a large saucepan over medium-high heat. Add the olive oil and heat to shimmering. Season all sides of the beef shin and veal shin with salt and pepper and arrange in a single layer in the pan. If they don't all fit at once, cook them in batches. Cook until well browned on all sides, about 8 minutes. Transfer to a plate when done and repeat with any remaining shins. Add the sausage and cook until well browned on all sides, about 5 minutes. Transfer to a plate when done.

2. Add the onion, garlic, and a large pinch of salt to the pan and cook, stirring occasionally, until the vegetables soften, about 5 minutes. Add the tomatoes (and juices) and then return the beef shin, veal shin, sausage, and any accumulated juices to the pan. Season with salt and pepper and bring the sauce to a boil. Reduce the heat to a gentle simmer, partially cover, and cook until the meat is tender, about 3 hours. If the sauce appears too thick while cooking, add ½ to 1 cup water.

3. When the Sunday sauce is ready, remove the beef shins and veal shins using a slotted spoon and set aside to cool. When cool enough to handle, pull the meat off the bone and roughly chop, then return it to the sauce.

4. Remove from the heat, add the cooked and drained cavatelli, and stir to combine. Divide among plates and serve with freshly grated parmesan and fresh basil, with Mom's Salad on the side.

Ricotta Cavatelli

Serves 4

2 cups whole-milk ricotta cheese
3 large eggs
Kosher salt

3 cups all-purpose flour, plus
 more for rolling

1. In a large bowl, combine the ricotta, eggs, and ½ teaspoon salt and stir to combine. Add the flour and mix by hand until the dough comes together into a ball. Add additional flour if the dough feels too sticky. Wrap in plastic and refrigerate for at least 1 hour and up to overnight.

2. Turn the dough out onto a lightly floured surface and knead it into a round. With a bench scraper or knife, cut the dough into quarters. Using your palms and fingers, gently roll each piece out to a ¼-inch-thick rope, adding flour when needed to prevent sticking. Cut each rope crosswise into ½-inch pieces. With a bench knife or butter knife, gently press down on each piece, beginning at the top and moving down toward the bottom, dragging your fingers toward you and causing the pasta to roll over onto itself. Transfer the formed pasta to a lightly floured sheet pan and let dry at room temperature for at least 30 minutes. (The pasta can be frozen at this point for up to 30 days, if desired.)

3. Add 2 tablespoons of salt to a medium pot of water and bring to a boil over high heat. Add the cavatelli and cook until they are al dente and float to the top, about 8 minutes, and drain the pasta.

Mom's Salad

Serves 4

2 tablespoons sour cream
¼ cup red wine vinegar
1 medium garlic clove, minced
1 teaspoon chopped fresh
 oregano
½ cup extra-virgin olive oil
2 heads romaine lettuce, cored
 and sliced crosswise

1 cucumber, large diced
2 tomatoes, cored and cubed or
 sliced into wedges
1 small red onion, halved and
 thinly sliced
Kosher salt and freshly ground
 black pepper

1. In a medium bowl, whisk together the sour cream, vinegar, garlic, oregano, and olive oil.

2. In a large bowl, combine the romaine, cucumber, tomatoes, and onions. Add dressing to taste, season with a pinch of salt and twist of pepper, and toss.

(recipe continues)

Meatballs

Makes 32 meatballs

½ cup cold beef stock
1 (¼-ounce) envelope unflavored
 gelatin powder
2 cups finely diced crustless soft
 bread
⅓ cup whole buttermilk
2 small yellow onions, finely
 chopped (about 1 cup)
4 ounces finely chopped
 pancetta (about ½ cup)
½ cup grated parmesan cheese

4 medium garlic cloves, minced
½ cup finely chopped fresh flat-
 leaf parsley
4 large egg yolks
1 tablespoon finely chopped fresh
 oregano
1 teaspoon ground fennel seeds
Kosher salt and freshly ground
 black pepper
1 pound ground beef (80% lean)
1 pound ground pork

1. Pour the beef stock into a small saucepan. Sprinkle the gelatin on top and let sit for 10 minutes to hydrate. Set the saucepan over medium heat and cook, while whisking, until the gelatin has dissolved, about 2 minutes. Transfer the mixture to a bowl and refrigerate until completely set, at least 30 minutes.

2. While the gelatin is setting, in a stand mixer fitted with the paddle, combine the bread and buttermilk. Blend on low to combine. Turn off the mixer and set aside to let the bread hydrate and soften for 10 minutes, then add the onions, pancetta, parmesan, garlic, parsley, egg yolks, oregano, and fennel seeds. Season with a pinch of salt and twist of pepper. Blend on low to combine.

3. Finely chop the chilled gelatin, add it to the bowl, and blend on low to combine. Add about one-third of the ground beef and one-third of the ground pork and blend on medium-high until thoroughly combined and paste-like, about 30 seconds. Remove the bowl from the stand mixer, add the remaining beef and pork, and fold in by hand until evenly incorporated.

4. Preheat the broiler to high heat. Line a sheet pan with foil.

5. Form the mixture into 32 equal meatballs about the size of a golf ball and place on the prepared sheet pan. Broil until golden brown on top, about 6 minutes.

Symon Says

The Sunday Sauce can be made up to 3 days in advance; wait until just before serving to add the broiled meatballs (the meatballs can be made 1 day ahead).

CAST-IRON SMASH BURGERS
+
DOUBLE-COOKED FRENCH FRIES
+
EXTRA-CRISPY ONION RINGS

Serves 4

You can't look at social media these days without watching someone making smash burgers. By smashing burgers onto hot steel, the beef develops a deeper flavor and gloriously crispy texture. You can use a portable griddle, a cast-iron griddle that goes right on the grill, or even a large cast-iron skillet. Make sure you let the griddle or skillet preheat until it's good and hot before adding the beef. For these, I like to use 80% lean ground beef because you want that extra fat—or "juice"—to keep the burgers moist even after smashing. Don't forget to toast the buns and let that cheese get good and melted. To make it the ultimate burger bash, we fry up some buttermilk-battered onion rings and extra-crispy French fries.

Special Sauce

½ cup mayonnaise (Duke's or Hellmann's)
2 tablespoons prepared horseradish
2 tablespoons ketchup
2 tablespoons Dijon mustard
1 tablespoon Worcestershire sauce
Hot sauce

Burgers

2 pounds ground beef (80% lean)
Kosher salt and freshly ground black pepper
Extra-virgin olive oil, for drizzling
2 small yellow onions, halved and very thinly sliced (about 1 cup)
16 slices American cheese

Serving

4 seeded potato rolls, split
12 pickle slices
Extra-Crispy Onion Rings (page 200)
Double-Cooked French Fries (page 200)

1. Make the special sauce: In a medium bowl, whisk together the mayonnaise, horseradish, ketchup, mustard, Worcestershire, and hot sauce to taste. Refrigerate until needed.

2. Preheat a gas or charcoal grill for indirect cooking, with one hot side and one hold (unheated) side. Set a large cast-iron skillet on the hot side of the grill to preheat.

3. Make the burgers: Divide the ground beef into 8 equal portions and roll them into balls. Season each one with a pinch of salt and twist of pepper. Add a drizzle of olive oil to the cast-iron pan. Arrange half of the onions in 4 even piles in the pan. Set a beef ball on top of each pile. Using a heavy metal spatula, smash each ball down to a thin patty. Cook until the beef and onions are golden brown and crisp, about 5 minutes. Flip the onion-crusted burgers, top each burger with 2 slices of cheese, and cook for 3 minutes. Move the burgers to the hold side of the grill while you repeat the process with the remaining onions and burgers.

4. To serve: Spread special sauce on the tops and bottoms of the rolls. Place pickle slices on the bottom halves, top with 2 burger patties each, extra-crispy onion rings, and then add the tops. Serve with French fries.

(recipe continues)

Double-Cooked French Fries

Serves 4

4 pounds russet potatoes, peeled
Neutral oil, for deep-frying (you'll
need about 2 quarts depending
on your pot)

Kosher salt

1. Cut the potatoes lengthwise into ½-inch-thick slabs, then cut the slabs lengthwise into ½-inch-thick sticks.

2. Line a large plate or platter with paper towels. Pour about 4 inches of oil into a deep-fryer or heavy-bottomed pot and heat to 325°F over medium-high heat.

3. Working in batches so as not to crowd the pan, fry the potatoes until light golden brown and almost cooked through, about 6 minutes. When done, remove the potatoes using a slotted spoon and drain on the paper towels.

4. Increase the oil temperature to 350°F.

5. When the oil is hot, working in batches again, fry the potatoes until golden brown and crisp, about 2 minutes. When done, remove the potatoes using a slotted spoon to a large bowl and immediately season with salt.

Extra-Crispy Onion Rings

Serves 4

½ cup all-purpose flour
2 teaspoons sweet paprika
1 teaspoon garlic powder
1 teaspoon onion powder
1 cup whole buttermilk

2 cups panko bread crumbs
Neutral oil, for frying
2 Vidalia onions, cut into ½-inch-
thick rings
Kosher salt

1. Put the flour in a shallow bowl and season with 1 teaspoon of the paprika, ½ teaspoon of the garlic powder, and ½ teaspoon of the onion powder. Put the buttermilk in a second shallow bowl. Put the panko in a third shallow bowl and season with the remaining 1 teaspoon paprika, ½ teaspoon garlic powder, and ½ teaspoon onion powder.

2. Line a large plate or platter with paper towels. Pour about 4 inches of oil into a deep-fryer or heavy-bottomed pot and heat to 360°F over medium-high heat.

3. Working with a few onion rings at a time, dredge the onions in the flour, making sure to coat all sides well. Shake off the excess. Dip the onions into the buttermilk, allowing the excess to drip off. Finally, lay the rings in the panko, turning and pressing to fully coat both sides.

4. When the oil is hot, working in batches so as not to crowd the pan, carefully add the battered onions to the oil and cook until golden brown and crispy, about 2 minutes. Remove using a slotted spoon and drain on the paper towels. Season with a few pinches of salt.

PORK TENDERLOIN SCHNITZEL
+
MUSHROOM GRAVY
+
CAULIFLOWER PUREE
+
CRISPY LEEKS

Serves 6

Schnitzel—fun to say, fun to eat. Every country seems to have its own distinct version of this thin breaded-and-fried food, whether it's beef, pork, or veal. This American-style schnitzel gets smothered in a hearty mushroom gravy that is perfect during the chilly months of the year—or whenever you need something rich and comforting. For the fried leeks, we toss them in Wondra flour before frying, which gives them the most amazing golden-brown and crispy exterior. I like to put the crispy fried leeks right on top for some great texture. The cauliflower puree is so easy, it practically cooks itself. It would go great with almost any meat or fish dish.

2 pounds pork tenderloin, trimmed of its silver skin
1 cup all-purpose flour
2 teaspoons sweet paprika
Kosher salt and freshly ground black pepper
5 large eggs

3½ cups panko bread crumbs
¼ cup vegetable oil, plus more if needed
Mushroom Gravy (page 204)
Cauliflower Puree (page 204)
Crispy Leeks (page 205)

1. Cut the tenderloin crosswise into 6 equal medallions. Place a piece of pork on a large sheet of plastic wrap and cover with a second sheet. Use a meat mallet to pound the pork to an even ⅛-inch thickness. Transfer to a plate while you repeat with the other pieces.

2. In a shallow bowl, combine the flour and 1 teaspoon of the paprika, season with a pinch of salt and twist of pepper, and stir to combine. Put the eggs in a second shallow bowl and beat them lightly. Put the panko and the remaining 1 teaspoon paprika in a third shallow bowl and stir to combine. Season both sides of the pork with salt and pepper. Working with one piece of meat at a time, dredge the pork in the flour, making sure to coat both sides well. Shake off the excess. Dip the pork into the beaten eggs, allowing the excess to drip off. Finally, lay the pork in the panko, turning and pressing to fully coat both sides.

3. Set a wire rack in a sheet pan. Set a large skillet over medium heat. Add the oil and heat to shimmering, then add one piece of pork. Cook until golden brown and crisp, about 1½ minutes per side. Transfer the pork to the wire rack. Repeat the process with the remaining pork, adding additional oil as needed.

4. Serve with the gravy, cauliflower puree, and leeks.

(recipe continues)

Mushroom Gravy

Makes 2½ cups

3 tablespoons extra-virgin olive oil

1 pound button mushrooms, quartered (about 3 cups)

4 tablespoons (½ stick) unsalted butter

1 small yellow onion, finely chopped (about ½ cup)

1 medium garlic clove, minced

Kosher salt and freshly ground black pepper

1 tablespoon finely chopped fresh thyme

¼ cup all-purpose flour

2 cups chicken stock

1 teaspoon Worcestershire sauce

1. Set a medium saucepan over medium-high heat. Add the olive oil and heat to shimmering, then add the mushrooms and cook, stirring only occasionally, until golden brown and crisp, about 5 minutes.

2. Add the butter and when melted add the onion and garlic. Season with a pinch of salt and twist of pepper. Add the thyme and flour and cook, stirring, for 1 minute. Whisking constantly, slowly add the stock. Bring the mixture to a boil, then reduce the heat to medium-low to maintain a gentle simmer. Cook, stirring occasionally, for 20 minutes.

3. Remove from the heat and stir in the Worcestershire sauce. Taste and adjust for seasoning, adding salt and pepper as needed.

Cauliflower Puree

Makes 3 cups

6 cups roughly chopped cauliflower

4 cups whole milk

1 teaspoon freshly grated nutmeg, plus more to taste

Kosher salt and freshly ground black pepper

4 tablespoons (½ stick) unsalted butter, at room temperature

1. In a large saucepan, combine the cauliflower, milk, and nutmeg and season with a pinch of salt and twist of pepper. Bring to a boil over medium-high heat. Reduce the heat to medium-low to maintain a gentle simmer, partially cover, and cook until the cauliflower is very tender, about 12 minutes. Scoop out and reserve ½ cup of the cooking liquid before draining the cauliflower in a colander.

2. Place the cauliflower in a blender or food processor, add the reserved cooking liquid and butter, and process until smooth, about 1 minute. Taste and adjust for seasoning, adding salt, pepper, and/or nutmeg as needed.

Crispy Leeks

Serves 6

2 leeks, white parts only
Vegetable oil, for frying

½ cup Wondra flour
Kosher salt

1. Cut the leeks in half lengthwise. Working in batches, cut the layers into thin matchsticks. Rinse the leeks in a bowl of cold water to clean. Drain, then blot dry with paper towels.

2. Line a large plate or platter with paper towels. Pour 4 inches of oil into a deep-fryer or deep heavy-bottomed pot and heat to 360°F over medium-high heat.

3. When the oil is hot, place the flour in a large bowl. Add the leeks and toss to thoroughly coat. Toss the leeks in a sieve or colander to remove excess flour. Working in batches so as not to crowd the pan, carefully add the leeks to the oil and cook until golden brown and crispy, about 1 minute. Remove using a slotted spoon and drain on the paper towels. Season with a few pinches of salt.

CHICKEN PAPRIKASH + SPAETZLE

Serves 4

In Cleveland, chicken paprikash is served all over town thanks to a large number of Eastern European restaurants. Frankly, without these places and their sublime comfort food, I'm not sure any of us would survive the long, cold winters. My pap made his own version of paprikash that the entire family loved and craved, and this is his recipe. It's enriched with sour cream at the end, which is nonnegotiable as far as I'm concerned. Also compulsory are (is?) the spaetzle, squiggly little dumplings that are the perfect paprikash sauce-delivery vehicle. Wait until the chicken is done cooking to start dropping the spaetzle into the boiling water so they can go straight into the sauce when done. This way, it all melds together like a great Italian pasta dish. The spaetzle-making process is straightforward and fun (if you ask me), but buttered noodles would be good here as well.

3 pounds bone-in, skin-on chicken thighs
Kosher salt and freshly ground black pepper
4 tablespoons sweet paprika
2 tablespoons chicken fat or unsalted butter
1 small yellow onion, sliced
½ head green cabbage, sliced
¼ cup all-purpose flour
4 cups chicken stock
Spaetzle (page 208)
1 cup sour cream, at room temperature
¼ cup finely chopped fresh flat-leaf parsley

1. Preheat the oven to 400°F.

2. Set a large Dutch oven over medium heat. Season the chicken on all sides with salt, pepper, and 1½ tablespoons of the paprika. Add the chicken fat to the pan and heat to shimmering, then add the chicken thighs skin-side down. Cook until golden brown and crisp, about 3 minutes. Flip and continue cooking until the other side is also nicely browned, about 3 minutes. Transfer to a plate.

3. To the same pan over medium heat, add the onion, cabbage, and the remaining 2½ tablespoons paprika. Season with a pinch of salt and twist of pepper. Cook, stirring occasionally, until the vegetables soften, about 5 minutes. Add the flour and cook, stirring, for 1 minute. Whisking constantly, slowly add the stock. Bring to a boil, then reduce the heat to medium-low to maintain a gentle simmer. Add the chicken skin-side up and any accumulated juices.

4. Transfer the pan to the oven and bake, uncovered, until the chicken reaches an internal temperature of 160°F, about 30 minutes.

5. When the chicken is almost done, cook the spaetzle.

6. Remove from the oven and stir in the spaetzle, sour cream, and parsley.

(recipe continues)

Spaetzle

Serves 4

4 large eggs
½ cup whole milk
2 tablespoons whole-grain
 mustard

Kosher salt and freshly ground
 black pepper
3 cups all-purpose flour

1. In a large bowl, whisk together the eggs, milk, and mustard. Season with a few pinches of salt and twists of pepper. Add the flour and stir to form a sticky batter. Cover and refrigerate for 30 minutes or up to 2 hours.

2. Add 2 tablespoons of salt to a medium pot of water and bring to a boil over high heat.

3. Lightly dampen a cutting board with water. Using a moistened rubber spatula, spread the chilled batter into a 3- to 4-inch-wide ribbon down the middle of the dampened board. Holding the cutting board over the edge of the pot, quickly cut and slide ¼-inch-wide pieces of the batter into the boiling water using a knife or bench scraper (you may have to cook the spaetzle in batches so as not to overcrowd the pot). When the spaetzle floats, after about 1 minute, cook for 30 seconds more. Remove the spaetzle from the water with a slotted spoon and add it directly to the chicken paprikash.

AMERICAN GOULASH

Serves 4 to 6

This is a Dennis Symon Special all the way. Think of this easy, economical, and comforting dish as a sort of homemade Hamburger Helper, but I've also heard it called American chop suey and even lazy Bolognese. Regardless what you call the dish, it was always a household favorite. If you like spicy food, add some fresh jalapeños, red pepper flakes, or a few shakes of your favorite hot sauce. Any small dried pasta would work here, such as farfalle, fusilli, or penne. I think after making this classic Symon supper you'll agree with my dad, who called it "cheap and cheerful."

Kosher salt
1 pound elbow macaroni
2 tablespoons extra-virgin
  olive oil
1 pound ground beef (80% lean)
Freshly ground black pepper
1 medium yellow onion, finely
  chopped
3 medium garlic cloves, minced

2 tablespoons fresh thyme, finely
  chopped
2 tablespoons tomato paste
1 (28-ounce) can crushed
  tomatoes
¼ cup freshly grated parmesan
  cheese (finely grated on a
  Microplane)

1. Add 2 tablespoons salt to a large pot of water and bring to a boil over high heat. Add the pasta and cook, stirring occasionally so it doesn't stick together, for 2 minutes less than the package directions. Reserving ½ cup of the pasta water, drain the pasta.

2. Set the same large pot over medium-high heat. Add the olive oil and heat to shimmering, then add the ground beef. Season with a pinch of salt and twist of pepper. Cook, stirring with a wooden spoon to break up the meat, until lightly browned, about 3 minutes. Add the onion, garlic, and thyme and cook, stirring occasionally, until the onion softens and begins to brown, about 5 minutes. Add the tomato paste and tomatoes, season with salt and pepper, and bring to a simmer. Add the drained pasta and reserved pasta water and continue cooking until slightly thickened, about 5 minutes.

3. Remove from the heat, stir in the parmesan, and serve.

CLASSIC MEATLOAF
+
ROOT VEGETABLE PUREE
+
CELERY SALAD

Serves 4 to 6

Back in culinary school, I once asked my professor what the difference was between pâté and meatloaf. After cursing me out in French, he said, "About $20." The truth is, meatloaf really is just a humble version of its fancy French cousin. We never ate it at home for some reason—instead, I discovered it while eating at friends' houses. Over the years, I began making my own versions, even with the "fancy" ketchup glaze! One of my moves to make mine shine is to mix in a whole head of roasted garlic, which adds a subtle sweetness. I like to serve the sliced meatloaf right on top of the root vegetable puree and then garnish it all with the celery salad.

Roasted Garlic

1 head garlic, intact, but loose papery skins removed
1 teaspoon extra-virgin olive oil

Glaze

1 cup ketchup
⅓ cup packed light brown sugar
3 tablespoons Worcestershire sauce
1 tablespoon Dijon mustard
1 tablespoon apple cider vinegar or sherry vinegar
Freshly ground black pepper

Meatloaf

2 pounds ground beef (80% lean)
2 large eggs, beaten
1 cup panko bread crumbs
2 small yellow onions, finely chopped (about 1 cup)
½ cup finely chopped fresh flat-leaf parsley
1 tablespoon Worcestershire sauce
1 teaspoon sweet paprika
½ teaspoon cayenne pepper
½ teaspoon Old Bay seasoning
Kosher salt and freshly ground black pepper

Serving

Root Vegetable Puree (page 215)
Celery Salad (page 215)

1. Roast the garlic: Preheat the oven to 400°F.

2. Slice the top ¼ inch off the garlic head to expose some of the cloves. Place the garlic head cut-side up in a large piece of foil, drizzle with the olive oil, and form a loose packet by gathering the foil up around the garlic. Place it directly on the oven rack and cook until the garlic is fragrant, golden brown, and soft, about 1 hour. Remove the packet from the oven, carefully open the foil, and set aside to cool. Leave the oven on but reduce the temperature to 375°F for the meatloaf.

(recipe continues)

Simply Symon Suppers

3. Meanwhile, make the glaze: In a medium bowl, whisk together the ketchup, brown sugar, Worcestershire, mustard, vinegar, and a few twists of black pepper.

4. Make the meatloaf: Line a sheet pan with foil.

5. In a large bowl, combine the ground beef, eggs, panko, onions, parsley, Worcestershire sauce, paprika, cayenne, and Old Bay seasoning. Squeeze the roasted garlic directly from the head into the bowl. Season with a few pinches of salt and twists of pepper. Mix to combine, being careful not to overwork the mixture. Using your hands, form the meat into the shape of a bread loaf. Place the loaf on the lined sheet pan and evenly coat the top and sides with the glaze.

6. Transfer to the oven and bake, uncovered, until the glaze is sticky, the loaf is golden brown, and the beef reaches an internal temperature of 160°F, about 1 hour.

7. Let the meatloaf stand for 5 minutes before slicing. Serve with the root vegetable puree and the celery salad.

Root Vegetable Puree

Serves 6

2 pounds russet potatoes, peeled and roughly chopped
2 pounds parsnips, peeled and roughly chopped
Kosher salt

1½ sticks (6 ounces) unsalted butter, at room temperature
½ teaspoon freshly grated nutmeg
Freshly ground black pepper

1. In a medium pot, combine the potatoes, parsnips, 2 tablespoons salt, and water to cover and bring to a boil over high heat. Reduce the heat to medium-low to maintain a gentle simmer and cook until the vegetables are easily pierced by a fork, about 20 minutes.

2. Drain the vegetables, return them to the pan, cover, and let sit for 5 minutes. Add the butter and nutmeg, season with a pinch of salt and twist of pepper, and mash until creamy, then use a whisk to whip the vegetables until smooth and fluffy.

Celery Salad

Serves 4

3 tablespoons extra-virgin olive oil
2 tablespoons white wine vinegar
1 tablespoon grainy mustard
1 tablespoon Dijon mustard
1 teaspoon honey
Kosher salt and freshly ground black pepper

4 celery stalks, thinly sliced (about 2 cups)
1 cup celery leaves
2 heads white Belgian endive, cut crosswise into ½-inch-thick rings

In a medium bowl, whisk together the olive oil, vinegar, grainy mustard, Dijon, and honey. Season with a pinch of salt and twist of pepper. Add the celery, celery leaves, and endive and toss to combine.

PORK MEATBALLS IN SAUERKRAUT

+

APPLE AND BRUSSELS SPROUTS SALAD

+

APPLE-PEAR SAUCE

Serves 6

Pork and sauerkraut is such a classic pairing that I decided to try braising pork meatballs in a savory blend of fresh apples and sauerkraut. The results are better than you can imagine, with the kraut bringing such distinctive flavors to the party. I may never serve meatballs in red sauce again! (Just kidding—I still do—as demonstrated in the Sunday Sauce!) Serve the apple salad and apple-pear sauce on the side and let everyone build their own plates for an interesting and affordable winter feast. Any leftover apple-pear sauce will stay good in the fridge for up to 2 weeks.

6 tablespoons extra-virgin olive oil
2 small yellow onions, finely chopped (about 1 cup)
2 medium garlic cloves, minced
Kosher salt
2 pounds ground pork
2 large eggs, beaten
1 cup panko bread crumbs
½ cup finely chopped fresh flat-leaf parsley
1 teaspoon celery seeds

1 teaspoon sweet paprika
¼ teaspoon cayenne pepper
Freshly ground black pepper
3 Granny Smith apples, peeled, cored, and diced
3 cups sauerkraut (I used Cleveland Kraut Gnar Gnar)
2 cups apple cider
Apple and Brussels Sprouts Salad (page 218)
Apple-Pear Sauce (page 218)

1. Set a large skillet over medium heat. Add 2 tablespoons of the olive oil and heat to shimmering, then add the onions, garlic, and a large pinch of salt. Cook, stirring occasionally, until the onions are soft, about 3 minutes. Set aside to cool.

2. In a large bowl, combine the pork, eggs, panko, parsley, celery seeds, paprika, cayenne, and cooled onion and garlic mixture. Season with a pinch of salt and twist of black pepper. Mix by hand until combined. Form the mixture into 12 equal meatballs. Each should be about the size of a golf ball.

3. Preheat the oven to 375°F.

4. Set a large Dutch oven over medium heat. Add the remaining 4 tablespoons olive oil and heat to shimmering. Working in batches, cook the meatballs until browned on all sides, about 5 minutes per batch. Transfer to a plate when done.

5. Carefully drain and discard all but 1 tablespoon of fat from the pan and set over medium heat. Add the apples and cook for 30 seconds. Add the sauerkraut and apple cider. Bring the sauce to a simmer and add the meatballs. Cover, transfer to the oven, and cook until the apples are soft and the meatballs are cooked through, about 30 minutes.

6. Serve the meatballs and sauerkraut with the apple salad and Brussels sprouts and apple-pear sauce on the side.

(recipe continues)

Apple and Brussels Sprouts Salad

Serves 6

3 tablespoons apple cider vinegar
2 teaspoons Dijon mustard
3 tablespoons extra-virgin olive oil
Kosher salt and freshly ground black pepper

2 apples, unpeeled and cut into matchsticks
4 cups shaved Brussels sprouts
½ cup thinly sliced scallions

In a medium bowl, whisk together the vinegar, mustard, and olive oil. Season with a pinch of salt and twist of pepper. Add the apples, Brussels sprouts, and scallions and toss to combine. Taste and adjust for seasoning, adding salt and pepper as needed.

Apple-Pear Sauce

Makes 4 cups

3 pounds apples, peeled, cored, and roughly chopped

1 pound Bartlett pears, peeled, cored, and roughly chopped
Juice of 1 lemon

In a medium saucepan, combine the apples, pears, and lemon juice. Cover and cook over low heat, stirring occasionally, until the fruit is very soft and has released its juices, about 15 minutes. Remove from the heat, transfer to a blender or food processor, and process until smooth.

> **Symon Says**
>
> The apple-pear sauce can be refrigerated for up to 5 days before serving.
> The meatball mixture can be made up to 1 day ahead of time.

STUFFED CABBAGE IN TOMATO SAUCE

Makes 12 to 14 rolls

Like chicken paprikash, stuffed cabbage was practically the official dish of Cleveland when I was growing up. Every household had its own special recipe, often handed down from one generation to the next. Like meatloaf, it's an inexpensive but delicious way to feed a large family or extended family. A lot of recipes use only the big outer leaves of the cabbage for the rolls, but that seems wasteful. I like to slice up the rest of the head and add it to the sauce. This is one of those dishes where the sum is greater than the parts: Every single element tastes so much better after cooking together in the oven. Just add some good-quality bread for mopping up the sauce and you're ready to go. This also goes great with a side of plain white rice. If you have leftovers—or feel like making an extra-big batch— these babies freeze well after they come out of the oven and cool a bit.

Kosher salt
1 large head green cabbage, cored

Tomato Sauce

3 tablespoons extra-virgin olive oil
1 small yellow onion, finely chopped
Kosher salt
1 tablespoon fresh thyme leaves
1 (14.5-ounce) can crushed tomatoes
6 cups spicy tomato-vegetable juice (such as Spicy Hot V8)
Freshly ground black pepper
¼ cup red wine vinegar

Filling

2 pounds ground beef (80% lean)
3 large eggs, slightly beaten
2 small yellow onions, finely chopped (about 1 cup)
½ cup bread crumbs
½ cup uncooked white rice
1 tablespoon chopped fresh thyme
2 tablespoons chopped fresh flat-leaf parsley
Kosher salt and freshly ground black pepper

Cooked white rice, for serving

1. Add 2 tablespoons salt to a large pot of water and bring to a boil over high heat. Carefully submerge the whole cabbage head cored-side down into the boiling water. As the large outer leaves become soft and pliable, remove them and transfer to a plate. When you have 12 to 14 large leaves, remove, drain, and reserve the rest of cabbage head.

2. Make the sauce: Set a large saucepan over medium-high heat. Add the olive oil and heat to shimmering, then add the onion and a pinch of salt. Cook, stirring occasionally, until the onion softens, about 5 minutes. Add the thyme and cook for 1 minute. Add the crushed tomatoes and tomato-vegetable juice. Season with a few pinches of salt and twists of pepper. Bring the sauce to a boil. Reduce the heat to medium-low to maintain a gentle simmer and cook, stirring occasionally, for 30 minutes. Remove from the heat and stir in the vinegar.

(recipe continues)

3. Make the filling: In a large bowl, combine the ground beef, eggs, onion, bread crumbs, rice, thyme, parsley, and 1 cup of the tomato sauce. Season with 2 teaspoons salt and a few twists of black pepper. Mix well to combine.

4. Preheat the oven to 350°F.

5. To stuff the cabbage, make a V-cut to remove (and discard) the thick stem portion on the cabbage leaves. Working with one cabbage leaf at a time, place a heaping ⅓ cup of the meat mixture near the stem end. Fold the bottom of the leaf over the filling, fold the two longer sides in over the filling, and give the roll one turn forward to form a burrito. Repeat with the remaining filling and cabbage leaves. When done, place the cabbage rolls seam-side down in 9 × 13-inch baking dish.

6. When the leftover cabbage head is cool enough to handle, thinly slice it and add it to the remaining tomato sauce. Pour the sauce on top of the cabbage rolls. Cover with foil and cook until the meat is cooked through and the rice is tender, about 1½ hours.

7. Remove from the oven and let stand for 15 minutes before serving with white rice.

BEEF STEW
+
POPOVERS
+
SHAVED CARROT SALAD

Serves 6

This hearty beef stew will get you through the darkest, coldest months of the year. Just having it on the stovetop, simmering the day away, is enough to brighten my mood. It fills the whole house with a heartwarming aroma that I think should be made into an air freshener! (You heard it here first.) Like any great stew, the key is to really take your time browning the meat. Don't crowd the pan—do it in batches if you need to—and let the beef develop some nice, deep color on it. Serving this stew with freshly baked popovers makes the meal even more special. I like to ladle the stew right over the airy rolls. The salad with shaved carrots and parsley leaves adds a nice bright crunch to the table. If you manage to not eat every single popover for dinner, serve them with butter and jam for breakfast. Any leftover vinaigrette can be stored in the fridge for up to 1 week.

½ cup all-purpose flour
1 teaspoon ground coriander
1 teaspoon ground cumin
1 teaspoon sweet paprika
½ teaspoon cayenne pepper
Kosher salt and freshly ground
    black pepper
2 pounds beef chuck or brisket,
    cut into 1½-inch cubes
⅓ cup extra-virgin olive oil

2 pounds mixed root vegetables
    (such as celery root, carrot,
    parsnip), peeled and roughly
    chopped
¼ cup tomato paste
8 cups beef stock
1 pound baby Yukon Gold
    potatoes, scrubbed
2 tablespoons finely chopped
    fresh rosemary
Popovers (page 226)
Shaved Carrot Salad (page 226)

1. In a large bowl, combine the flour, coriander, cumin, paprika, and cayenne. Season with a pinch of salt and twist of black pepper and whisk to combine.

2. Season the beef on all sides with salt and pepper. Dredge the meat in the flour mixture, making sure to coat all sides well. Shake off the excess.

3. Set a large Dutch oven over medium-high heat. Add the olive oil and heat to shimmering, then arrange half of the beef in an even layer in the pan. Cook, turning occasionally, until well browned on all sides, about 12 minutes. Transfer to a plate and repeat the process with the remaining beef.

4. To the same Dutch oven, add the mixed root vegetables and a pinch of salt. Cook, stirring occasionally, until the vegetables soften and begin to brown, about 8 minutes. Add the tomato paste and cook, stirring occasionally, until the paste begins to darken, about 1 minute. Add the stock, potatoes, rosemary, beef, and any accumulated juices. Season with a pinch of salt and twist of black pepper and bring to a boil. Reduce the heat to medium-low to maintain a gentle simmer and cook, partially covered, until the meat and vegetables are tender, about 1½ hours.

5. Serve with popovers and the carrot salad.

(recipe continues)

Popovers

4 large eggs
1½ cups whole milk
1 teaspoon kosher salt

1½ cups all-purpose flour
¼ cup meat drippings or
extra-virgin olive oil

1. Preheat the oven to 425°F. Place a 12-cup muffin tin in the oven to preheat.

2. In a blender or food processor, combine the eggs, milk, salt, and flour. Blend on high until completely smooth, about 30 seconds. Let the batter rest for 30 minutes.

3. Remove the muffin tin from the oven and carefully, and evenly, divide the fat among all 12 cups. Return the tin to the oven for 2 minutes. Remove the tin from the oven and fill each cup one-third of the way with batter. Bake until golden brown and puffy, about 15 minutes.

4. Serve immediately.

Shaved Carrot Salad

Serves 4

3 tablespoons extra-virgin
olive oil
2 tablespoons red wine vinegar
1 tablespoon Dijon mustard
1 teaspoon honey
Kosher salt and freshly ground
black pepper

3 cups peeled carrot slices, very
thinly sliced on an angle
1 small red onion, thinly sliced
(about ½ cup)
½ cup fresh flat-leaf parsley
leaves

In a medium bowl, whisk together the olive oil, vinegar, mustard, and honey. Season with a pinch of salt and twist of pepper. Add the carrots, onion, and parsley and toss to combine.

CHICKEN POT PIE
+
SHAVED MUSHROOM SALAD

Serves 6

Is there anybody out there who doesn't love chicken pot pie? It is such an American classic. In my house, I rarely roast just one whole chicken at a time. It's not much more work or time to cook two at once, and that all but guarantees that there will be plenty of perfectly cooked meat for recipes like this one. If you're in a pinch for time, you can always pick up a rotisserie bird from the market. As far as the recipe goes, just use it as a guide and have fun with it. You can add or swap in sweet potatoes, parsnips, or celery root. You can even make this with leftover Thanksgiving turkey! I know a lot of people don't love raw mushrooms, but I think shaving them super-thin is a game changer. No worries if mushrooms aren't your thing; the Kohlrabi and Green Apple Salad (page 243), Shaved Brussels Sprout Salad (page 141), or Roasted Radicchio Salad with Pecans (page 157) would all work great here.

2 pounds boneless, skinless chicken thighs, cut into 1-inch pieces
Kosher salt and freshly ground black pepper
2 tablespoons extra-virgin olive oil, plus more if needed
8 tablespoons (1 stick) unsalted butter
2 medium garlic cloves, minced
¼ teaspoon crushed red pepper flakes
3 tablespoons all-purpose flour
2 cups chicken stock
1 cup heavy cream
1 cup dry white wine

¼ cup dry sherry
2 small russet potatoes (about ½ pound), peeled and diced
3 medium carrots (about ½ pound), peeled and diced
1 medium yellow onion, diced
1 fresh bay leaf
½ cup fresh or frozen peas
1 (10 × 15-inch) sheet frozen puff pastry, thawed
Egg wash: 1 large egg beaten with 1 tablespoon heavy cream
Shaved Mushroom Salad (page 230)

1. Set a large Dutch oven over medium-high heat. Season the chicken on all sides with salt and black pepper. Add the olive oil to the pan and heat to shimmering, then add the chicken in an even layer. Cook, turning occasionally, until well browned on all sides, about 7 minutes. If the chicken doesn't all fit at once, cook it in batches (with additional olive oil, if needed). If browned in batches, return all the chicken and any accumulated juices to the pan when done.

(recipe continues)

2. To the same pan, add the butter, garlic, and pepper flakes and cook, stirring, for 1 minute. Add the flour and cook, stirring, for 1 minute. Constantly stirring, slowly add the stock, cream, wine, and sherry. Bring to a boil, then reduce the heat to medium-low to maintain a gentle simmer. Add the potatoes, carrots, onion, and bay leaf, partially cover, and cook, stirring occasionally, until the vegetables are very soft and the chicken is cooked through, about 20 minutes. Season with a pinch of salt and twist of black pepper. Remove from the heat and stir in the peas.

3. Preheat the oven to 400°F.

4. Carefully pour the pot pie mixture into a 9-inch deep-dish round pie dish. Using kitchen shears, cut a 9-inch round piece of puff pastry and place it on top. (Discard the remaining puff pastry or save for another purpose.) Brush the puff pastry with the egg wash. Transfer to the oven and bake until puffy and golden brown, about 20 minutes.

5. Remove from the oven and let sit for 5 minutes before serving with the mushroom salad.

(recipe continues)

Shaved Mushroom Salad

Serves 4

2 tablespoons red wine vinegar
Juice of 1 lemon
1 medium garlic clove, minced
2 teaspoons Dijon mustard
⅓ cup extra-virgin olive oil
2 teaspoons fresh oregano, finely chopped
Kosher salt and freshly ground black pepper

3 cups shaved trumpet mushrooms (cremini work, too)
4 celery stalks, very thinly sliced (about 2 cups)
1 cup celery leaves
⅓ cup 1-inch lengths fresh chives
⅓ cup fresh flat-leaf parsley leaves
Flaky sea salt, for serving

1. In a medium bowl, whisk together the vinegar, lemon juice, garlic, and mustard. Whisking constantly, slowly add the olive oil. Add the oregano, season with a pinch of kosher salt and twist of pepper, and stir to combine.

2. In a large bowl, combine the mushrooms, celery, celery leaves, chives, and parsley. Add dressing to taste and toss to combine. Transfer to a platter, sprinkle with sea salt, and serve.

POTATO AND SWEET POTATO PANCAKES
+
POACHED EGGS
+
PEAR AND CRISPY-QUINOA SALAD

Serves 4

Potato pancakes are so delicious and versatile, which is probably why my dad enjoyed making them so often. It's fun to mix in different types of spuds and root veggies, like these sweet potatoes, but also carrots, parsnips, and rutabagas. While fried or scrambled eggs work great, I think these poached beauties placed right on top of the crispy pancake make the dish a bit more elegant. The pear and crispy quinoa salad gets tossed in an amazing pear vinaigrette. Any leftover dressing can be refrigerated for up to 1 week.

1 large russet potato, scrubbed and grated on the large holes of a box grater
1 large sweet potato, peeled and grated on the large holes of a box grater
1 small onion, peeled and grated on the large holes of a box grater
2 large eggs
¼ cup matzo meal

2 tablespoons thinly sliced fresh chives
Kosher salt and freshly ground black pepper
2 tablespoons extra-virgin olive oil
Applesauce, for serving
Poached Eggs (page 234)
Pear and Crispy-Quinoa Salad (page 235)

1. Wrap the grated potato, sweet potato, and onion in a kitchen towel and wring the vegetables out over a small bowl to remove as much of the liquid as you can. Set the liquid aside. Transfer the vegetables to a medium bowl, add the eggs, matzo meal, and chives. Season with a pinch of salt and twist of pepper and toss to combine.

2. The starch from the potato will have settled to the bottom of the small bowl, so carefully pour out and discard the extracted vegetable water on top, leaving the starch behind. Add the starch to the potato-egg mixture and toss to combine.

3. Line a large plate or platter with paper towels. Set a large nonstick skillet over medium-high heat. Add 1 tablespoon of the olive oil and heat to shimmering, then add enough of the potato mixture to make 4 medium pancakes (about half of the mixture). Cook, without disturbing, until golden brown, about 4 minutes per side. Reduce the heat if the potatoes are browning too quickly. Transfer to the paper towels to drain. Repeat the process with the remaining 1 tablespoon olive oil and the remaining potato mixture.

4. Serve immediately with applesauce, poached eggs, and the pear and quinoa salad.

(recipe continues)

Poached Eggs

Serves 4

2 tablespoons distilled white
vinegar

4 large eggs

1. In a medium saucepan, combine 4 cups water and the vinegar and bring to a strong simmer over medium-high heat.

2. Crack each egg into its own little bowl. With a spoon, create a large (but gentle) whirlpool in the simmering water by stirring in one direction around the perimeter of the pan. Gently lower the eggs one at a time into the center of the pan.

3. Poach, untouched, until the eggs are set enough to be lifted out of the water without breaking but the yolks are still runny, about 3 minutes.

4. Gently lift the eggs out of the water with a slotted spoon and transfer to a paper towel to remove excess water.

Pear and Crispy-Quinoa Salad

Serves 4

½ cup quinoa, rinsed
Kosher salt
2 ripe Bartlett or Anjou pears, halved, cored, and roughly chopped (about 1 cup)
2 tablespoons Champagne vinegar
2 teaspoons Dijon mustard
1 teaspoon honey
3 tablespoons extra-virgin olive oil

2 tablespoons thinly sliced fresh chives
Freshly ground black pepper
4 heads Little Gem lettuce, cored and separated into leaves (Bibb or any type of leafy lettuce works, too)
⅓ cup roasted whole unsalted almonds, roughly chopped
½ cup crumbled feta cheese
½ cup pomegranate seeds

1. Line a sheet pan with parchment paper.

2. In a medium saucepan, combine ¾ cup water, the quinoa, and a pinch of salt. Bring to a boil over medium-high heat. Stir the quinoa, reduce the heat to medium-low to maintain a gentle simmer, partially cover, and cook until the quinoa pops open and all the liquid is absorbed, about 15 minutes.

3. Spread the quinoa out onto the prepared sheet pan to cool and dry for 15 minutes.

4. Preheat the oven to 375°F.

5. Transfer the pan of quinoa to the oven and toast for 20 minutes. Stir and continue cooking until crispy, about 10 minutes longer.

6. In a blender, combine the pears, vinegar, mustard, honey, and olive oil and process until smooth. Transfer to a bowl, add the chives, season with a pinch of salt and twist of pepper, and stir to combine.

7. Put the lettuce in a large bowl, add dressing to taste, and toss to coat. Transfer to a platter and top with the almonds, feta, pomegranate seeds, crispy quinoa, and freshly ground black pepper.

FRENCH ONION SOUP + WHEAT BERRY, ROASTED SQUASH, AND SHAVED BRUSSELS SPROUTS SALAD

Serves 6

It's crazy how a few humble ingredients like onions and beef stock can be transformed into one of the world's most delicious soups. All it takes is time, patience, and a good bit of stirring. The key to this dish is the long, gentle cooking, which turns the onions into sweet, golden-brown flavor bombs. Of course, French onion soup isn't French onion soup without the toasted bread and melted Gruyère cheese, which drips down the side of the bread and into the soup. All this soup needs to turn it into the perfect cold-weather meal is a nice salad. This one is a knockout—chewy, nutty, and healthy with wheat berries.

Small bunch of fresh thyme
2 fresh bay leaves
6 tablespoons extra-virgin olive oil
4 tablespoons (½ stick) unsalted butter
10 large yellow or white onions, halved and thinly sliced (about 10 cups)
3 medium garlic cloves, minced
Kosher salt

2 tablespoons all-purpose flour
1 cup dry red wine
6 cups beef stock
Freshly ground black pepper
1 baguette, cut on an angle into about 12 (1-inch-thick) slices
12 slices Gruyère cheese
Wheat Berry, Roasted Squash, and Shaved Brussels Sprouts Salad (page 238)

1. Bundle up the thyme and bay leaves in butcher's twine and set aside.

2. Set a large Dutch oven over medium heat. Add 2 tablespoons of the olive oil and the butter and heat to shimmering, then add the onions, garlic, and a large pinch of salt. Cook, stirring occasionally, until the onions soften and begin to brown, about 5 minutes. Reduce the heat to low and continue cooking, stirring frequently to prevent scorching, until the onions are deeply caramelized, at least 30 minutes.

3. Add the flour and cook, stirring, for 1 minute. Add the wine and deglaze the pan, scraping with a wooden spoon to loosen the browned bits on the bottom of the pan. Add the beef stock and herb bundle. Season with a pinch of salt and twist of pepper. Bring the soup to a boil. Reduce the heat to medium-low to maintain a gentle simmer, partially cover, and cook for 30 minutes.

4. Meanwhile, preheat the oven to 375°F.

5. Arrange the baguette slices on a sheet pan, brush with the remaining 4 tablespoons olive oil, and season with salt and pepper. Bake, flipping halfway, until golden brown and crisp, about 10 minutes.

6. Preheat the broiler to high.

7. Arrange the baguette slices on a sheet pan in pairs that touch. Top each pair with 2 slices of the Gruyère. Place under the broiler and cook until the cheese is melted and golden brown, about 2 minutes.

8. Remove and discard the herb bundle. Ladle the soup into six bowls, top each bowl with a cheese toast, and serve with the wheat berry salad.

(recipe continues)

Wheat Berry, Roasted Squash, and Shaved Brussels Sprouts Salad

Serves 4

1 small butternut squash, peeled, seeded, and medium diced (about 2 cups)
½ cup plus 1 teaspoon extra-virgin olive oil
Kosher salt and freshly ground black pepper
1 cup apple cider
2 fresh bay leaves
1½ cups wheat berries, rinsed
¼ cup sherry vinegar

2 teaspoons honey
1 teaspoon Dijon mustard
Grated zest and juice of 1 orange
½ pound Brussels sprouts, thinly shaved (about 2 cups)
¼ cup roasted, salted pistachios
½ cup fresh flat-leaf parsley, roughly torn
Shaved parmesan cheese, for serving

1. Preheat the oven to 425°F. Line a sheet pan with foil.

2. Arrange the squash in an even layer on the sheet pan. Drizzle with 1 teaspoon of the olive oil and season with a pinch of salt and twist of pepper. Cook until the squash softens and browns around the edges, about 20 minutes.

3. Meanwhile, in a medium saucepan, combine 2 cups water, the cider, bay leaves, and a good pinch of salt. Bring to a boil over medium-high heat. Stir in the wheat berries, reduce the heat to medium-low to maintain a gentle simmer, partially cover, and cook until tender, about 25 minutes. Drain, discard the bay leaves, and set aside to cool.

4. In a large bowl, whisk together the vinegar, remaining ½ cup olive oil, the honey, mustard, orange zest, and orange juice. Season with a pinch of salt and twist of pepper. Add the Brussels sprouts, pistachios, parsley, roasted squash, and drained wheat berries and toss to combine. Taste and adjust for seasoning, adding salt and pepper as needed.

5. Top with shaved parmesan.

> Symon Says
>
> The wheat berries for the salad and the soup can both be cooked and refrigerated up to 2 days ahead of time.
>   When ready to serve, warm the soup and finish with the bread component, then finish assembling the salad.

PIEROGI "LASAGNA" CASSEROLE

+

KOHLRABI AND GREEN APPLE SALAD

Serves 10 to 12

Imagine all the comforting flavors and textures of potato and cheese pierogies, but without all that filling and crimping work. Here, all those classic components—tender dough, buttery mashed potatoes, sautéed onions—are layered into a lasagna-like casserole. I admit that this is cheating, but when the end results are this tasty, nobody is going to call you out on it. Even my pap, who was a little offended the first time I made it for him, came around after the first or second bite. I think kohlrabi is an underrated vegetable in this country. It's crisp, sweet, and mildly bitter, making it the perfect addition to wholesome salads like this one.

Pierogi Dough

8 tablespoons (1 stick) unsalted butter, at room temperature
¾ cup sour cream
1 large egg
1 tablespoon thinly sliced fresh chives
1 teaspoon kosher salt
2 cups all-purpose flour, plus more for rolling

Lasagna Fillings

2 pounds russet potatoes, peeled and cut into large chunks
Kosher salt
1 cup heavy cream
8 tablespoons (1 stick) cold unsalted butter, cubed

1½ cups farmer cheese
Freshly ground black pepper
1 tablespoon extra-virgin olive oil
1 pound bacon, chopped
2 large yellow onions, thinly sliced

Assembly

Softened butter, for the baking dish
All-purpose flour, for rolling out
1½ cups shredded Gruyère cheese

Serving

Sour cream
Thinly sliced fresh chives
Kohlrabi and Green Apple Salad (page 243)

1. Make the pierogi dough: In a large bowl, combine the butter, sour cream, egg, chives, and salt and mix by hand, being careful not to overwork the dough. Add the flour and mix by hand until the dough comes together into a ball. Wrap in plastic and refrigerate for at least 2 hours and up to 2 days.

2. Make the lasagna fillings: In a medium pot, combine the potatoes, 2 tablespoons salt, and water to cover and bring to a boil over high heat. Reduce the heat to medium-low to maintain a gentle simmer and cook until easily pierced by a fork, about 20 minutes.

3. When the potatoes are almost done cooking, heat the cream in a small saucepan over medium heat.

(recipe continues)

4. Drain the potatoes and return them to the pan. Add the butter and hot cream a little at a time while pressing with a potato masher. Continue adding the butter and cream, while mashing, until it all has been incorporated. Whisk in the farmer cheese. Season with a pinch of salt and twist of pepper.

5. Set a large skillet over medium-high heat. Add the olive oil and heat to shimmering, then add the bacon. Cook, stirring occasionally, until the bacon is crisp, about 10 minutes.

6. To the same skillet, add the onions and season with a pinch of salt and twist of pepper. Cook, stirring frequently, until the onions are well browned, about 8 minutes. Remove from the heat and set aside to cool.

7. Assemble the lasagna: Preheat the oven to 350°F. Grease a 9 × 13-inch baking dish with butter.

8. On a lightly floured surface, roll out the dough to a 24 × 13-inch piece about ⅛ inch thick. Use a knife or pizza cutter to make 6 equal strips that measure 4 × 13 inches. Add 2 tablespoons salt to a large pot of water and bring to a boil over high heat. Add two strips of dough to the water and cook for 2 minutes. Remove to a sheet pan while you repeat the process with the remaining dough strips.

9. Arrange 2 dough strips on the bottom of the prepared baking dish. Top the dough with one-third of the mashed potatoes and smooth them into an even layer with a spatula. Add 2 more strips of cooked dough followed by another third of the mashed potatoes. Scatter the surface with the remaining onions and bacon. Add 2 more strips of cooked dough followed by the remaining mashed potatoes, smoothing them into an even layer with a spatula. Top with the Gruyère.

10. Bake, uncovered, until the lasagna is golden brown and bubbling, about 25 minutes.

11. Remove from the oven and let sit for 10 minutes before slicing. Serve topped with sour cream and chives, with the kohlrabi salad on the side.

Kohlrabi and Green Apple Salad

Serves 4

½ cup extra-virgin olive oil
¼ cup white wine vinegar
1 teaspoon Dijon mustard
1 teaspoon honey
Kosher salt and freshly ground
    black pepper
3 medium kohlrabi, thinly sliced
    into matchsticks (about 3 cups)

4 medium Granny Smith apples,
    halved, cored, and cut into
    matchsticks (about 3 cups)
2 tablespoons thinly sliced fresh
    chives
2 tablespoons finely chopped
    fresh dill

In a medium bowl, whisk together the olive oil, vinegar, mustard, and honey. Season with a pinch of salt and twist of pepper. Add the kohlrabi, apples, chives, and dill and toss to combine.

Holidays

Around here, we like to treat every day like a special occasion, because nobody is getting any younger! But growing up, it was the decadent, multicourse holiday meals that I looked forward to the most, often starting the countdown days or even weeks in advance. These festive and extravagant meals would take place either at our house or over at my grandparents' house, and they always revolved around the kitchen and dining room table. Many of my fondest memories were forged during the Thanksgivings, Easters, and Christmases of the '70s and '80s.

Like those memories, it's impossible to pick a favorite holiday dish. Mom's lasagna, turkey with Pap's corn pudding, and smoked prime rib with horseradish sauce would all satisfy me on my deathbed. Now that I'm doing the bulk of the cooking, I don't see any reason why those glorious meals need to be reserved for just one day out of the year. Celebrate Christmas in July or Thanksgiving in March. Life's too short to postpone celebrating with family and friends over a great meal.

PASTRAMI-SMOKED PRIME RIB
+
BROWN BUTTER WHIPPED POTATOES
+
CHARRED BRUSSELS SPROUTS
+
HORSE-RADISH SAUCE

Serves 6

For me, this meal is pure luxury from start to finish. Prime rib is one of the most indulgent foods out there, but when it is slow smoked over charcoal—or better still, over wood—it somehow manages to taste even better. Serve it with classic horseradish sauce and I promise you that every carnivore at the table will be begging for seconds. Liz demands that I make these buttery whipped potatoes for practically every holiday meal—and yes, they do require *that* much butter! Cooking the butter until it just begins to brown adds an amazing nutty richness to the potatoes. I like to blast my Brussels sprouts in a really hot oven to caramelize them, which adds a pleasant sweetness. You don't need an expensive smoker to make this (or any smoked foods); if you have an ordinary kettle grill, you can use the snake method to produce consistent, steady heat. You can also prepare the beef in an oven using the same temperatures and it will still be amazing.

½ cup coarsely cracked black peppercorns
½ cup coarsely cracked coriander seeds
¼ cup coarsely cracked mustard seeds
¼ cup kosher salt
2 tablespoons crushed red pepper flakes

1 (4-pound) prime rib
2 cups apple- or cherrywood chips, for smoking
Brown Butter Whipped Potatoes (page 250)
Charred Brussels Sprouts (page 253)
Horseradish Sauce (page 253)

1. In a small bowl, whisk together the black peppercorns, coriander, mustard seeds, salt, and pepper flakes. Liberally season the roast on all sides and set aside.

2. Prepare a charcoal grill with the "snake method" by mounding and overlapping three or four unlit briquettes on the bottom charcoal grate around the perimeter of the grill base. Place wood chips or chunks on top of the unlit coals at regular intervals to generate smoke throughout the entire process. Light a chimney half-filled with charcoal. When burning white-hot, carefully pour the coals onto one end of the briquette circle to ignite the snake.

3. When the temperature in the smoker reaches 325°F, place the meat in the center of the grill, cover, and cook until the beef reaches an internal temperature of 125°F for rare to 135°F for medium, depending on your desired doneness, about 3½ hours. For the best results, use a probe thermometer to continually monitor the meat's temperature.

4. Transfer the beef to a cutting board and let rest for 20 to 30 minutes. Slice to the desired thickness and serve with the whipped potatoes, Brussels sprouts, and horseradish sauce.

(recipe continues)

Brown Butter Whipped Potatoes

Serves 4 to 6

Kosher salt
2 pounds russet potatoes, peeled and cut into 2-inch chunks
8 tablespoons (1 stick) unsalted butter, cut into tablespoons

½ cup whole milk
¼ cup freshly grated parmesan cheese (finely grated on a Microplane)
Freshly ground black pepper

1. In a large pot, combine 2 tablespoons salt, the potatoes, and water to cover. Bring to a boil over high heat. Reduce the heat to medium-low to maintain a gentle simmer and cook until the potatoes are very tender, about 25 minutes. Drain, return the potatoes to the pot, and cover.

2. In a large skillet, melt the butter over medium heat and cook, stirring, until the butter begins to brown and smell nutty, about 5 minutes. Be careful not to let the butter burn. Remove from the heat.

3. Add the brown butter to the potatoes. Using a potato masher, mash the potatoes until smooth. Add the milk and whisk to blend. Add the parmesan and whisk until the cheese is fully incorporated and the potatoes are airy. Taste and adjust for seasoning, adding salt and pepper as needed.

Symon Says

The pastrami spice mix can be mixed and stored at room temperature in an airtight container for up to 1 week ahead of using.
The horseradish sauce can be made up to 3 days ahead of time.
The prime rib can be seasoned with the spice mix up to 2 days ahead of time and kept tightly wrapped and refrigerated until ready to cook. Let it sit out at room temperature for 45 minutes to 1 hour before smoking.

(recipe continues)

Simply Symon Suppers

Charred Brussels Sprouts

Serves 4

1 pound Brussels sprouts, ends trimmed, halved
4 tablespoons extra-virgin olive oil
Kosher salt and freshly ground black pepper
2 tablespoons red wine vinegar

2 tablespoons Pickled Mustard Seeds (page 149) or Old Brooklyn Mustards' Original IPA
2 tablespoons thinly sliced fresh chives
1 teaspoon honey

1. Position a rack in the bottom third of the oven and preheat to 500°F.

2. Place the Brussels sprouts on a sheet pan, drizzle with 1 tablespoon of the olive oil, and season with a few pinches of salt and twists of pepper. Toss to evenly coat and then arrange cut-side down in a single layer. Cook until charred and just tender, about 8 minutes.

3. Meanwhile, in a medium bowl, whisk together the vinegar, mustard seeds, and the remaining 3 tablespoons olive oil. Season with a pinch of salt and twist of pepper. Add the chives and stir to combine.

4. Drizzle the Brussels sprouts with honey, top with the vinaigrette, and toss to combine.

Horseradish Sauce

Makes 1⅓ cups

⅓ cup whole buttermilk
⅓ cup prepared horseradish
⅓ cup mayonnaise
⅓ cup sour cream
2 tablespoons thinly sliced fresh chives

1 teaspoon kosher salt
1 tablespoon freshly ground black pepper
1 medium garlic clove, grated

In a medium bowl, whisk together the buttermilk, horseradish, mayonnaise, sour cream, chives, salt, pepper, and garlic. The sauce can be made 3 days in advance.

CORNED BEEF AND CABBAGE
+
IRISH SODA BREAD

Serves 4 to 6

Although my sister, Nikki, dreams of being Irish, our family is 100 percent *NOT* Irish. That said, so many of our closest friends in Cleveland are indeed Irish, and some of their cherished family recipes became some of our favorites, too. When it comes to Celtic feasts, it's hard to beat this classic pairing of corned beef and cabbage with soda bread, which I typically bust out for St. Patrick's Day. Katie absolutely nailed the soda bread, which also happens to go great with your morning coffee (especially when schmeared with lots of Irish butter). To make the variation sometimes referred to as spotted dog, substitute raisins for the caraway seeds.

1 (12-ounce) bottle lager beer
½ cup whole-grain mustard
1 head green cabbage, sliced
1 yellow onion, sliced
3 medium garlic cloves, sliced
2 teaspoons toasted caraway seeds
Kosher salt and freshly ground black pepper

1 (3-pound) corned beef brisket
2 pounds baby Yukon Gold potatoes
3½ tablespoons Bertman Original Ballpark Mustard
Freshly grated horseradish, for serving
Irish Soda Bread (page 257)

1. In a large Dutch oven, stir together 2 cups water, the beer, and whole-grain mustard. Add the cabbage, onion, garlic, and caraway seeds and stir to combine. Season with a pinch of salt and twist of pepper. Position the corned beef fat-side up on top of the vegetables. Bring to a boil, then reduce the heat to medium-low to maintain a gentle simmer, cover, and cook for 2 hours.

2. Add the potatoes and continue cooking until the corned beef and potatoes are tender, about 2 hours more. Transfer the meat to a cutting board and let rest for 10 minutes before slicing.

3. To the cabbage in the Dutch oven, add the ballpark mustard and stir to combine. Taste and adjust for seasoning, adding salt and pepper as needed.

4. Slice the corned beef against the grain, garnish with horseradish, and serve with the cabbage and potatoes. Have soda bread on the side.

(recipe continues)

Irish Soda Bread

Makes 1 large round loaf

3½ cups all-purpose flour
¼ cup sugar
1 teaspoon baking powder
1 teaspoon baking soda
¾ teaspoon kosher salt
2 sticks (8 ounces) cold unsalted
    butter, preferably Irish butter,
    cut into small cubes

1 cup sour cream
2 tablespoons caraway seeds or
    1½ cups dark raisins
1 large egg
1 cup whole buttermilk

1. Position a rack in the center of the oven and preheat to 375°F. Line a cast-iron skillet with parchment paper.

2. In a large bowl, whisk together the flour, sugar, baking powder, baking soda, and salt. Add the cold butter and cut it in by hand or using a pastry cutter until the mixture resembles coarse sand with small marbles of butter remaining. Place the bowl in the freezer for 15 minutes.

3. Remove the bowl from the freezer, add the sour cream, and mix with a fork to make a shaggy dough. Stir in the caraway seeds (or raisins).

4. In a small bowl, whisk together the egg and buttermilk.

5. Form a well in the flour-butter mixture, add the egg-buttermilk mixture, and stir with a fork until a slightly wet dough forms. Transfer the dough to the prepared skillet. Using floured hands, shape the dough into a round loaf 8 inches across and 2 inches tall. With a sharp knife, score a ¾-inch-deep cross onto the top of the dough to ensure even baking.

6. Bake until light golden brown and a toothpick inserted into the center comes out clean, about 45 minutes.

7. Allow to cool before slicing.

> **Symon Says**
>
> Soda bread can be made, formed, and kept tightly wrapped and refrigerated up to 1 day ahead of baking. Alternately the bread can be baked and cooled up to 2 days ahead of time.

SMOKED HAM WITH BOURBON GLAZE
+
HASH BROWNS AND CHEDDAR CASSEROLE
+
GREEN BEAN CASSEROLE

Serves 6

Yum—I'm already dreaming about all the sandwiches that I'll make with the leftover ham! While I typically reserve smoked ham for the big holidays, there's no rule that says you can't make this showstopper any day of the year. In my opinion, there's still nothing more comforting and delicious than a well-constructed casserole. This hash brown and cheddar version is over-the-top hearty and gratifying. Growing up in the Midwest, it wasn't a holiday without a green bean casserole. So yes, this is a two-casserole holiday meal—and I doubt any of your guests is going to complain about it! My recipe ditches the ubiquitous can of soup for a made-from-scratch creamy mushroom gravy and swaps the bland store-bought fried onions for delectable just-fried shallots.

2 cups apple cider
1 cup pure maple syrup
½ cup bourbon
8 tablespoons (1 stick) unsalted butter
Grated zest and juice of 1 orange
1 (10-pound) fully cooked spiral-sliced ham

2 cups apple or cherry wood chips (optional, if smoking)
Hash Browns and Cheddar Casserole (page 261)
Green Bean Casserole (page 262)

1. In a medium saucepan, combine the apple cider, maple syrup, and bourbon. Bring the sauce to a boil over medium heat. Reduce the heat to medium-low to maintain a gentle simmer and cook for 10 minutes. Add the butter and orange juice and continue cooking until the mixture reduces to a thin glaze, about 15 minutes. Remove the glaze from the heat and stir in the orange zest.

To make the ham in the oven

2. Preheat the oven to 325°F.

3. Place the ham in a large roasting pan, brush with half of the glaze, cover the pan tightly with foil, and cook until warmed through, about 1 hour.

4. Increase the oven temperature to 425°F. Remove the foil, baste the ham with the remaining glaze, and continue cooking, uncovered, until deeply caramelized, about 15 minutes more. Let rest loosely tented with foil for 10 minutes before serving.

(recipe continues)

To make the ham in the smoker

2. Preheat a lump charcoal grill for indirect cooking, with one hot side and one hold (unheated) side. Place a handful of apple- or cherrywood chips directly onto the hot coals, creating a smoker effect.

3. Place the ham directly on the grate over the hold side, coat with half of the glaze, cover, and cook until warmed through, about 45 minutes.

4. Move the ham to the hot side and continue cooking, basting it with some of the glaze every few minutes, until deeply caramelized, about 20 minutes. If the ham is getting too caramelized on one side, turn it to another side. Let rest loosely tented with foil for 10 minutes before serving.

To serve

5. Serve the ham with the hash brown casserole and the green bean casserole.

Symon Says

The bourbon glaze can be made and refrigerated up to 3 days ahead of time.

The mushroom broth for the green bean casserole can be made up to 3 days ahead of time.

If you want to take it a step further, make the mushroom gravy using the broth. Refrigerate up to 2 days and, when ready to serve, warm over medium heat before adding the green beans and proceeding with the recipe.

Hash Browns and Cheddar Casserole

Serves 4 to 6

1 tablespoon unsalted butter
2 medium garlic cloves, minced
Kosher salt
2 (12-ounce) cans evaporated milk
1 cup sour cream
2 tablespoons fresh thyme leaves

3 dashes hot sauce
3 pounds russet potatoes, scrubbed and grated
2 cups grated cheddar cheese
Freshly ground black pepper
4 scallions, white and light-green parts only, thinly sliced

1. Preheat the oven to 400°F.

2. In an enameled Dutch oven, melt the butter over medium heat. Add the garlic and a pinch of salt and cook, stirring occasionally, until the garlic softens, about 3 minutes. Add the evaporated milk, sour cream, thyme, and hot sauce and stir to combine. Bring to a simmer and stir in the potatoes and 1 cup of the cheddar. Season with a pinch of salt and twist of pepper. Use a spatula to spread the potatoes into an even layer.

3. Cover, transfer to the oven, and bake until the potatoes are just about cooked through, about 20 minutes.

4. Top with the remaining 1 cup cheddar, cover, and continue baking until the potatoes are cooked through and the cheese has melted, about 10 minutes.

5. Top with the scallions and let rest for 5 minutes before serving.

(recipe continues)

Green Bean Casserole

Serves 6

Mushroom Gravy

2 pounds mixed fresh mushrooms
 and mushroom stems
1 ounce mixed dried mushrooms
4 tablespoons (½ stick) unsalted
 butter
3 medium garlic cloves, minced
1 tablespoon roughly chopped
 fresh thyme
Kosher salt
½ cup all-purpose flour
1 tablespoon sherry vinegar
1 tablespoon Worcestershire
 sauce

Casserole

Softened unsalted butter, for the
 casserole dish
Kosher salt
2 pounds green beans, ends
 trimmed
Freshly ground black pepper
¼ cup panko bread crumbs

Fried Shallots

Canola oil, for deep-frying
½ cup all-purpose flour
½ cup cornstarch
Kosher salt
4 shallots, very thinly sliced

1. Make the mushroom gravy: In a large soup pot, combine the mushrooms, mushroom stems, dried mushrooms, and 10 cups cold water. Bring to a gentle boil over medium-high heat. Reduce the heat to low to maintain a gentle simmer, partially cover, and cook until reduced by half, about 2 hours. Strain the mushroom broth (discard the solids).

2. In a large saucepan, melt the butter over medium heat. Add the garlic, thyme, and a pinch of salt. Cook until the garlic softens, about 1 minute. Add the flour and cook, whisking, for 1 minute. Whisking constantly, slowly add the mushroom broth, then bring the sauce to a boil. Reduce the heat to medium-low to maintain a gentle simmer and cook, stirring occasionally, until slightly reduced and thickened, about 30 minutes.

3. Remove from the heat, stir in the vinegar and Worcestershire sauce, and transfer the mushroom gravy to a large bowl.

4. For the casserole: Preheat the oven to 400°F. Grease an enameled casserole dish with butter.

5. Fill a large bowl with ice water. Add 2 tablespoons of salt to a large pot of water and bring to a boil over high heat. Add the beans and cook until just tender but still crisp, about 2 minutes. Drain and immediately add to the bowl of ice water to stop the cooking and preserve the color.

6. Drain the beans, add them to the bowl of mushroom gravy, and toss to thoroughly coat. Season with a pinch of salt and twist of pepper and then transfer to the prepared casserole dish. Top with the panko.

7. Transfer to the oven and bake, uncovered, until golden brown and bubbling, about 30 minutes.

8. Meanwhile, make the fried shallots: Line a large plate or platter with paper towels. Pour 4 inches canola oil into a deep-fryer or deep heavy-bottomed pot and heat to 370°F over medium-high heat.

9. In a large bowl, combine the flour, cornstarch, and a pinch of salt and whisk to blend.

10. When the oil is hot, add the shallots to the flour mixture and toss to thoroughly coat, making sure to separate the shallots into rings. Toss the shallots in a sieve or colander to remove excess flour. Working in batches so as not to crowd the pan, carefully add the shallots to the oil and fry until golden brown and crispy, about 1 minute. Remove using a slotted spoon and drain on the paper towels. Season with a few pinches of salt.

11. Remove the casserole from the oven and top with the fried shallots.

MOM'S OTHER LASAGNA + MOZZARELLA-STUFFED GARLIC BREAD

Serves 6 (with leftovers)

Angel, my mom, is the undisputed Queen of Lasagna. She has multiple variations based largely on whether she will be including meat, but also depending on what she happens to have on hand. It doesn't matter what she uses or doesn't use, the lasagnas always come out amazing. Of all her lasagna recipes, this is my absolute favorite—and the one we feature at Angeline, the Atlantic City restaurant I named after her. It's layered with Bolognese and béchamel and is reminiscent of the style of lasagna you most often find in Italy. Mom often paired the dish with homemade mozzarella-stuffed garlic bread, an irresistible loaf of buttery cheese-filled bread balls. This combo is definitely one of my desert-island meals.

Noodles

Kosher salt
2 (1-pound) boxes lasagna
  noodles

Meat Sauce

Small bunch of fresh thyme
¼ cup extra-virgin olive oil
1 pound ground beef (80% lean)
1 large yellow onion, finely
  chopped
2 celery stalks, finely chopped
3 medium garlic cloves, thinly
  sliced
Kosher salt
3 tablespoons tomato paste
1 cup dry white wine
2 (28-ounce) cans crushed
  tomatoes
Freshly ground black pepper

Cheese Sauce

6 tablespoons unsalted butter
½ cup all-purpose flour
2½ cups whole milk
1 teaspoon freshly grated nutmeg
Kosher salt and freshly ground
  black pepper
2 pounds whole-milk ricotta
  cheese
1 cup freshly grated pecorino or
  parmesan cheese (finely grated
  on a Microplane)
2 large egg yolks

Assembly and Serving

1 cup shredded low-moisture
  mozzarella cheese
Mozzarella-Stuffed Garlic Bread
  (page 269)

1. Cook the noodles: Add 2 tablespoons salt to a large pot of water and bring to a boil over high heat. Add the pasta and cook, stirring occasionally so it doesn't stick together, for 2 minutes less than the package directions. Drain the noodles in a colander and arrange on a sheet pan to cool.

2. Make the meat sauce: Bundle up the thyme in butcher's twine and set aside.

3. Set a large skillet over medium-high heat. Add the olive oil and heat to shimmering, then add the ground beef. Cook, stirring with a wooden spoon to break up the meat, until lightly browned, about 3 minutes. Add the onion, celery, garlic, and a large pinch of salt and cook, stirring occasionally, until the vegetables soften and begin to brown, about 5 minutes. Add the tomato paste and cook, stirring occasionally, until the paste begins to darken, about 1 minute. Add the wine, tomatoes, and thyme bundle and cook, partially covered, until the sauce has thickened,

(recipe continues)

about 20 minutes. Remove and discard the herb bundle and season with a pinch of salt and twist of pepper.

4. Make the cheese sauce: In a large saucepan, melt the butter over medium heat. Add the flour and cook, whisking, for 1 minute. Whisking constantly, slowly add the milk. Bring the sauce to a boil, then reduce the heat to medium-low to maintain a gentle simmer. Add the nutmeg, 1 teaspoon salt, and a few twists of black pepper. Cook, stirring frequently, until thickened and smooth, about 10 minutes. Remove from the heat and whisk in the ricotta, pecorino, and egg yolks until thoroughly blended.

5. Preheat the oven to 375°F. Line a sheet pan with foil.

6. Assemble the lasagna: Spread 1 cup of the meat sauce evenly over the bottom of a large roasting or lasagna pan. Arrange a layer of 6 noodles across the bottom of the pan, slightly overlapping them, and gently press them into the sauce. Top the noodles with 1½ cups meat sauce and then 1½ cups cheese sauce and smooth it into an even layer with a spatula. Arrange another layer of 6 overlapping noodles, pressing them down gently. Top the noodles with another 1½ cups of the meat sauce, followed by 1½ cups cheese sauce. Repeat this noodle, meat sauce, cheese sauce process two more times. For the final layers, arrange another layer of 6 overlapping noodles followed by any remaining cheese sauce and then any remaining meat sauce. Top with the mozzarella.

7. Coat a piece of foil with cooking spray and set it, sprayed-side down, over the lasagna, crimping down the foil's edges. Place the baking dish on the foil-lined sheet pan and bake until completely warmed through, about 1 hour.

8. Uncover the lasagna and continue cooking until golden brown and crusty, about 25 minutes.

9. Remove from the oven and let rest for 45 minutes before slicing. Serve with the mozzarella-stuffed garlic bread.

Symon Says

The meat sauce and cheese sauce can each be made and refrigerated up to 2 days ahead of time. When ready to assemble, heat each sauce over medium-low heat to warm through, then proceed as instructed.

Mozzarella-Stuffed Garlic Bread

Serves 6

Dough

3 cups bread flour
2 tablespoons honey
2 tablespoons unsalted butter, at room temperature
1 (2¼-teaspoon) envelope instant yeast
1½ teaspoons kosher salt

Garlic Bread

6 tablespoons unsalted butter
2 tablespoons extra-virgin olive oil
2 medium garlic cloves, grated
1 tablespoon finely chopped fresh rosemary
½ teaspoon garlic powder
Cooking spray
16 (1-inch) cubes low-moisture mozzarella cheese
¼ cup freshly grated parmesan cheese (finely grated on a Microplane)

1. Make the dough: In a stand mixer fitted with the dough hook, combine the bread flour, honey, butter, yeast, and salt. Blend on low while adding 1 cup lukewarm water. Continue blending on low until the dough comes together into a mass, about 2 minutes. Increase the speed to medium and knead until the dough is smooth and silky, about 10 minutes. Turn the dough out into a lightly greased bowl, cover with plastic, and let rise until doubled in size, about 1 hour.

2. Make the garlic bread: In a small saucepan, combine the butter, olive oil, grated garlic, rosemary, and garlic powder and cook, stirring occasionally, over medium-low heat until aromatic, about 2 minutes. Remove from the heat and set aside.

3. Grease a Bundt pan or tube pan with cooking spray.

4. On a clean (unfloured) surface, divide the dough into 16 equal portions (about 1½ ounces each). Press a cube of cheese into each piece, fold the dough up and around it, and shape it into a ball. Dip a ball into the butter/garlic/oil mixture, making sure to completely coat it, and then place the ball into the prepared pan. Repeat with the remaining dough balls. Pour any of the remaining butter/garlic/oil mixture evenly over the bread and top the balls with the parmesan. Cover with plastic and let rise until doubled in size, about 45 minutes.

5. About 30 minutes before the bread is risen, preheat the oven to 400°F.

6. Remove the plastic and bake until golden brown and the bread is cooked all the way through, about 30 minutes.

7. Remove from the oven and let stand in the pan for 5 minutes before inverting onto a plate.

CLASSIC SYMON TURKEY
+
PAP'S CORN PUDDING
+
TURKEY GRAVY
+
CLASSIC DRESSING

Serves 10

Does anybody else think it's strange that we only eat turkey on Thanksgiving? Other than turkey breast from the deli counter, we completely ignore this delicious food 364 days a year (not counting leftovers, of course!). Turkey is actually one of the most economical meats out there, and there are a million different ways to prepare it, such as roasted, smoked, deep-fried—you name it. These days, everybody wants you to brine your bird, but I've been doing it the same way for thirty years, ever since my grandfather showed me the butter-soaked cheesecloth method. I promise you that this is the easiest and most consistent way to cook your turkey. Pap also knocked the side dishes out of the park, like his epic corn pudding that famously (or perhaps infamously) started with a box of Jiffy corn muffin mix. It's so ridiculously easy that you'll probably feel guilty from all the compliments. Make it once and I guarantee it will become a holiday staple. When it comes to the dressing, I have tried all the cheffy tricks like buying fancy bread and drying it out, but nothing beats the prepackaged stuffing cubes. Trust me, I'll never go back—and neither will you! And it wouldn't be a turkey dinner without ladle after ladle of rich, silky gravy made from the flavorful drippings.

1 (12-pound) turkey, cavity cleaned
3 yellow onions, quartered
Small bunch of fresh thyme
8 tablespoons (1 stick) unsalted butter
½ cup chicken stock
5 sprigs fresh thyme or sage

1 tablespoon extra-virgin olive oil, plus more for the turkey
Kosher salt and freshly ground black pepper
Pap's Corn Pudding (page 273)
Turkey Gravy (page 273)
Classic Dressing (page 275)

1. Take the turkey out of the refrigerator 1 to 2 hours before cooking to let it come to room temperature.

2. Position a rack in the bottom third of the oven and preheat to 425°F.

3. Place 4 of the onion quarters and the thyme bunch inside the turkey cavity.

4. In a medium saucepan, combine the butter, stock, and thyme sprigs and bring to a simmer over medium heat. Remove from the heat until cool enough to handle.

(recipe continues)

5. Meanwhile, add the remaining 8 onion quarters to a large roasting pan. Drizzle with the 1 tablespoon olive oil and season with salt and pepper. Coat the turkey with more olive oil and season inside and out with salt and pepper. Place the turkey on top of the onions. If you have the turkey neck, add that to the pan as well.

6. When the butter mixture is cool enough to handle, submerge a double layer of cheesecloth large enough to cover the turkey in the mixture and drape it over the breast and legs. Pour the remaining butter sauce and herbs all over the bird. Push the herb sprigs to the bottom of the pan.

7. Transfer to the oven and roast for 45 minutes. Reduce the oven temperature to 375°F. Continue roasting until the leg meat reaches an internal temperature of 160°F, about 3 hours. For the best results, use a probe thermometer to continually monitor the turkey's temperature.

8. Transfer the turkey to a carving board and remove and discard the cheesecloth. Reserve the pan drippings in the roasting pan for the Turkey Gravy (opposite). Let the turkey rest for 30 minutes before carving and serving.

9. Serve the turkey with gravy, corn pudding, and dressing.

Symon Says

The corn pudding batter can be mixed up to a day ahead of time. When ready to serve, remove from the fridge 30 minutes prior to baking to take the chill off, pour the batter into your baking vessel, and bake.

The dressing can be assembled up to 1 day ahead of time. When ready to serve, remove from the fridge 30 minutes prior to baking to take the chill off then proceed with the recipe.

The gravy can be made up to 3 days ahead of time. When ready to serve, reheat over medium-low heat and add any pan drippings from the turkey before serving.

Pap's Corn Pudding

Serves 8

3 sticks (12 ounces) unsalted butter, melted, plus more for the baking dish
3 (8.5-ounce) boxes Jiffy corn muffin mix
5 cups corn kernels, fresh or thawed frozen
3 (14.75-ounce) cans cream-style corn
2 cups sour cream
1 cup mascarpone cheese
4 large eggs
4 scallions, white and light-green parts only, thinly sliced (about ½ cup)

1. Preheat the oven to 350°F. Grease a 9 × 13-inch baking dish with butter.

2. In a large bowl, whisk together the melted butter, corn muffin mix, corn kernels, cream-style corn, sour cream, mascarpone, eggs, and scallions. Pour the mixture into the prepared baking dish.

3. Transfer to the oven and bake, uncovered, until golden brown on top and just set in the center, about 50 minutes. Let stand for 5 minutes before serving.

Turkey Gravy

Makes 1 quart

4 tablespoons (½ stick) unsalted butter
2 small yellow onions, finely chopped (about 1 cup)
1 medium carrot, chopped (about ½ cup)
1 celery stalk, chopped (about ½ cup)
Kosher salt and freshly ground black pepper
Small bunch of fresh thyme
1 bay leaf
¼ cup all-purpose flour
4 cups turkey or chicken stock
Reserved drippings from roasting a turkey, strained
Roasted turkey neck (if you have one)
1 teaspoon aged balsamic vinegar
1 teaspoon Worcestershire sauce

1. In a large heavy-bottomed soup pot, melt the butter over medium-high heat. Add the onions, carrot, celery, and a large pinch of salt. Cook, stirring occasionally, until the vegetables are aromatic and lightly browned, about 10 minutes.

2. Add the thyme, bay leaf, and flour and stir to fully coat the vegetables. Whisking constantly, slowly add the stock and reserved drippings from the roasting pan. Add the roasted turkey neck if you have one. Bring the sauce to a boil. Reduce the heat to medium-low to maintain a gentle simmer and cook, stirring occasionally, for 45 minutes. Taste and adjust for seasoning, adding salt and pepper as needed.

3. Strain through a fine-mesh sieve into a saucepan (discard the solids). Stir in the vinegar and Worcestershire sauce. Taste and adjust for seasoning, adding more Worcestershire and/or vinegar as needed.

(recipe continues)

Classic Dressing

Serves 8

Olive oil or softened butter, for the baking dish

1 tablespoon extra-virgin olive oil

2 pounds loose breakfast sausage

4 tablespoons (½ stick) unsalted butter

2 large yellow onions, finely chopped (about 2 cups)

2 celery stalks, finely chopped (about 1 cup)

½ teaspoon celery seeds

½ teaspoon crushed red pepper flakes

Kosher salt

2 tablespoons finely chopped fresh sage

1 tablespoon finely chopped fresh thyme

3 cups low-sodium chicken or turkey stock

16 cups packaged stuffing bread cubes

¾ cup roughly chopped fresh flat-leaf parsley

Freshly ground black pepper

1. Preheat the oven to 375°F. Grease a large enameled casserole dish.

2. Set a large skillet over medium-high heat. Add the olive oil and heat to shimmering, then add the sausage. Cook, stirring with a wooden spoon to break up the meat, until golden brown and crispy, about 5 minutes. Add the butter, onions, celery, celery seeds, pepper flakes, and a large pinch of salt. Cook, stirring occasionally, until the vegetables are aromatic and soft, about 5 minutes. Add the sage and thyme and cook for 30 seconds. Add the stock and bring to a simmer.

3. In a large bowl, combine the bread cubes, sautéed vegetable mixture, and parsley. Season with a pinch of salt and twist of pepper and toss to thoroughly combine.

4. Transfer the stuffing mixture to the prepared casserole dish, cover with foil, and cook until warmed through, about 35 minutes. Remove the foil and cook until the top is golden brown and crispy, about 15 minutes. Let set for 10 minutes before serving.

Desserts

When it came to developing the recipes for this chapter, I leaned pretty heavily on Katie Pickens, who is an absolute pastry wizard. Together we came up with a selection of killer desserts that meet my strict requirements: simple, not overly sweet, and definitely not too finicky or complicated. I don't like fluff!

For this cookbook, the desserts also had to be inspired by my own personal experiences. Some, like the Ricotta Cornmeal Pound Cake (page 281), come from my first "real" chef job in Cleveland. Others, like the Baklava (page 290), stretch clear back to my earliest memories cooking alongside my mom. I couldn't imagine writing a family-inspired cookbook without including Dad's Death by Chocolate (page 286) and Pap's Pretzel Crust Cheesecake Squares (page 294), but we also added fresh, contemporary treats like the Berry Balsamic Crisp (page 282), which is loaded with the ripest seasonal fruit you can find at the farmers' market. Don't forget a big scoop of vanilla ice cream!

RICOTTA CORNMEAL POUND CAKE

Makes 1 loaf

This dessert was inspired by my first real restaurant job after graduating from culinary school. At Players in Cleveland, we served this type of cake with a pear compote and fresh whipped cream. It was simple and fantastic. Like that classic recipe, this one dials back the sweetness to let the cornmeal and ricotta shine. This cake goes great with whatever fruit jam or preserves you happen to have on hand.

Cooking spray, for the pan
1 cup all-purpose flour
1 cup finely ground yellow cornmeal
1¾ teaspoons baking powder
½ teaspoon kosher salt
10 tablespoons unsalted butter, at room temperature

1 cup sugar
2 large eggs
1 large egg yolk
¼ cup full-fat Greek yogurt
Grated zest of 1 orange
1 cup whole-milk ricotta cheese
2 teaspoons pure vanilla extract
Jam, for serving

1. Preheat the oven to 325°F. Line the bottom of a loaf pan with parchment paper and mist the pan with cooking spray.

2. In a medium bowl, whisk together the flour, cornmeal, baking powder, and salt.

3. In a stand mixer fitted with the paddle, beat the butter and sugar until pale and fluffy, about 5 minutes. Add the whole eggs and egg yolk and beat until fully incorporated. Add the yogurt, orange zest, and flour mixture and mix until well blended, stopping once or twice to scrape down the sides and bottom of the bowl. Add the ricotta and vanilla and mix until blended.

4. Pour the batter into the prepared loaf pan. Transfer to the oven and bake until a toothpick inserted into the center comes out clean, about 1 hour.

5. Allow to cool in the pan before slicing and serving with your favorite jam.

BERRY BALSAMIC CRISP

Serves 6

I love a great baked-fruit dessert. Lucky for me, both Liz and Katie make amazing ones, especially crisps: simple, old-fashioned desserts designed to showcase whatever ripe, seasonal fruit happens to be making an appearance at the market. The fruit gets capped with a buttery, crumbly topping and baked until bubbling and golden brown. In a pinch, frozen fruit will do, but it's a weak substitute for the real thing. All this dish needs to reach its full potential is a big scoop of vanilla bean ice cream. The addition of balsamic vinegar might sound odd, but it adds a subtle depth of flavor and sweetness that really makes a difference.

Softened butter, for the pan

Filling

3 cups blueberries, blackberries, or a mix
3 cups raspberries
3 cups strawberries, quartered
⅓ cup all-purpose flour
⅓ cup granulated sugar
Grated zest of 1 lemon
3 tablespoons aged balsamic vinegar

Topping

¾ cup all-purpose flour
¾ cup old-fashioned rolled oats
½ cup packed light or dark brown sugar
½ cup granulated sugar
1 teaspoon ground cinnamon
Pinch of salt
8 tablespoons (1 stick) cold unsalted butter, cut into small cubes

1. Preheat the oven to 375°F. Grease a 10-inch ovenproof skillet with butter.

2. Make the filling: In a medium bowl, combine the blueberries, raspberries, strawberries, flour, granulated sugar, lemon zest, and vinegar and gently toss to combine. Transfer to the buttered skillet and arrange in an even layer.

3. Make the topping: In a large bowl (or in a stand mixer bowl), combine the flour, oats, brown sugar, granulated sugar, cinnamon, and salt and stir to blend. Add the cold butter and cut it in using a pastry cutter (or the stand mixer paddle) until you have a coarse crumb and the flour is fully hydrated.

4. Sprinkle this mixture evenly and loosely over the top of the berries. Transfer to the oven and bake, uncovered, until golden brown, crisp, and bubbling, about 35 minutes. Remove from the oven and let stand at least 10 minutes before serving.

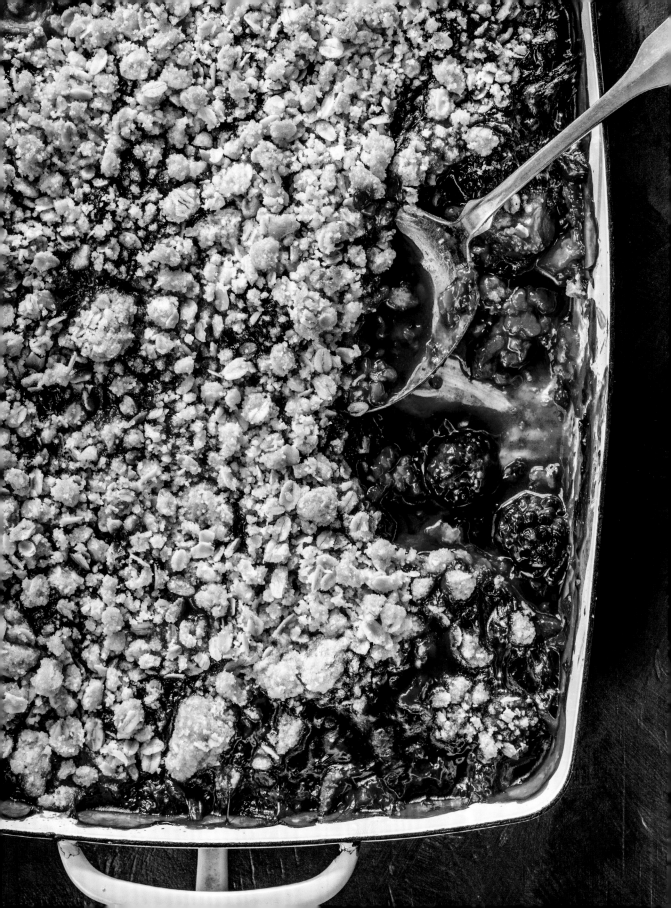

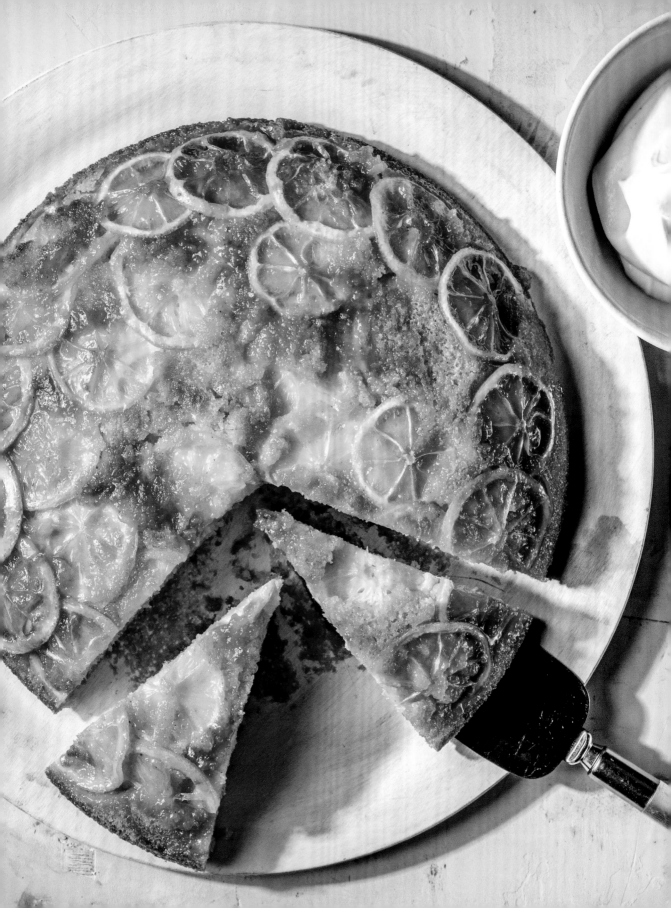

BROWN BUTTER LEMON UPSIDE-DOWN CAKE

Serves 8

This is an uncomplicated cake that comes across as elegant and impressive. It's not too heavy, not too rich, and not too sweet, which makes it a hit in my book. Though it's an attractive dessert as is, there's no rule against topping it with some fresh seasonal berries when serving. After the cake goes into the oven, place a mason jar with a tight-fitting lid into the freezer. If you've never made whipped cream this way, prepare to have your world rocked!

Cake

2 cups all-purpose flour
1½ teaspoons kosher salt
½ teaspoon baking powder
½ teaspoon baking soda
Pinch of ground cinnamon
1¼ cups whole milk
1 cup extra-virgin olive oil
1 cup granulated sugar
3 large eggs
1 teaspoon pure vanilla extract

3 lemons, 1 zest and juiced, 2 very thinly sliced and seeded
4 tablespoons (½ stick) unsalted butter
¾ cup packed light brown sugar

Whipped Cream

1 cup heavy cream, well chilled
2 tablespoons powdered sugar
1 teaspoon pure vanilla extract

1. Preheat the oven to 350°F.

2. Make the cake: In a medium bowl, whisk together the flour, salt, baking powder, baking soda, and cinnamon.

3. In a large bowl, whisk together the milk, olive oil, sugar, eggs, vanilla, lemon zest, and lemon juice. Add the flour mixture and whisk to combine.

4. In a shallow enameled Dutch oven, melt the butter over medium heat. Swirl the butter around the pan and up the sides while it melts. When the butter begins to brown and smell nutty, add the brown sugar and whisk until it dissolves. The mixture will resemble wet sand and won't get completely smooth.

5. Remove the pan from the heat and neatly arrange the lemon slices in an overlapping pattern across the entire bottom (which will become the top). Scrape in the cake batter.

6. Transfer to the oven and bake until a toothpick inserted in the center of the cake comes out dry, about 50 minutes. Remove from the oven and let cool for 5 minutes, then carefully invert the cake onto a platter and let cool until ready to serve.

7. Meanwhile, make the whipped cream: Place a 16-ounce mason jar in the freezer for 1 hour or up to overnight.

8. Remove the mason jar from the freezer. Pour in the cream and add the powdered sugar and vanilla. Screw on the top and shake vigorously until the cream has very soft peaks, about 5 minutes.

9. Slice the cake into 8 wedges, top each with a dollop of whipped cream, and serve.

DAD'S DEATH BY CHOCOLATE

Serves 8

My dad will be the first to admit that this recipe title is a bit of an exaggeration. As far as we know, this dessert has not killed a single family member or friend who consumed it. And it's not for a lack of opportunity, because, let me tell you, hardly a holiday went by without him making this delicious trifle. In fact, if anybody was at risk of bodily harm, it would be my dad if he didn't make his special dessert. The entire family goes crazy for this decadent, creamy chocolate dessert layered with crunchy chocolate wafer cookies.

Chocolate Pudding

4 large egg yolks
1½ cups granulated sugar
4 cups heavy cream
1 teaspoon kosher salt
1 cup unsweetened cocoa powder
⅓ cup all-purpose flour
8 tablespoons (1 stick) unsalted butter, cubed
1 cup bittersweet chocolate chips

Assembly

4 cups heavy cream, well chilled
¼ cup powdered sugar
½ cup crème fraîche
3 cups crumbled chocolate wafer cookies
Four (1.4-ounce) bars chocolate-covered English toffee, such as Heath, chopped

1. Make the chocolate pudding: In a medium bowl, whisk together the egg yolks and granulated sugar. Add the cream and the salt and whisk to combine. In a separate medium bowl, whisk together the cocoa and flour. Add the cream mixture to the flour mixture and whisk to combine. Scrape into a medium saucepan.

2. Set the saucepan over medium heat and bring the mixture to a simmer, stirring constantly so it doesn't burn on the bottom or in the corners of the pan. Remove from the heat, add the butter and chocolate chips, and stir until melted and smooth. Set aside to cool.

3. To assemble: In a stand mixer fitted with the whisk (or in a large bowl using a hand mixer), combine the cream and powdered sugar and whisk until soft peaks are formed. Gently fold in the crème fraîche.

4. In a large trifle bowl, add about half of the chocolate pudding. Top with about half of the whipped cream mixture. Sprinkle on half of the crumbled cookies and half of the chopped toffee candy. Repeat this process, finishing with a layer of the cookies and candy. Cover and refrigerate for at least 2 hours before serving. The trifle will keep for up to 3 days.

BAKLAVA

Makes one 9 × 13-inch pan

One of my earliest cooking memories is of me and my mom making baklava. I believe I was around eight years old and it was my job to dab the sheets of phyllo with melted butter. I remember going as fast as I could and still not being able to keep up! My mother excelled at pretty much everything she attempted in the kitchen, but if I had to pick her masterpiece, it would be baklava. I must have sampled thousands of different versions of baklava over the years, and to this day, I have never tasted one better than hers.

Syrup

¾ cup sugar
½ cup honey
1 tablespoon fresh lemon juice
1 orange peel slice

Baklava

1 cup graham cracker crumbs
1 cup roasted, salted pistachios
1 cup walnuts
1 teaspoon ground cinnamon
¼ teaspoon kosher salt
1 (16-ounce) package 9 × 14-inch Athens phyllo dough, thawed if frozen
3 sticks (12 ounces) unsalted butter, melted

1. Make the syrup: In a medium saucepan, combine ⅓ cup water, the sugar, honey, and lemon juice and bring to a gentle boil, whisking frequently. Reduce the heat to low, add the orange peel, and let simmer, without stirring, for 15 minutes. Remove from the heat to cool and thicken while assembling the baklava.

2. Preheat the oven to 350°F.

3. Assemble the baklava: In a food processor, combine the graham cracker crumbs, pistachios, walnuts, cinnamon, and salt and pulse until coarsely chopped, about 10 times. Transfer to a bowl and set aside.

4. Unroll the entire package of phyllo dough. Throughout the assembly process, keep the stack of phyllo dough covered with a damp towel to prevent it from drying out.

5. Grease a 9 × 13-inch baking pan with some of the melted butter. Position one sheet of phyllo in the bottom of the pan and brush the entire surface with butter. Repeat the process with 9 more sheets of phyllo. Arrange half of the crumb/nut mixture evenly across the surface of the top sheet and gently press into the dough. Repeat the phyllo/butter process with 4 more sheets. Arrange the remaining nut mixture evenly across the surface of the top sheet. Repeat the phyllo/butter process with 10 more sheets. Using a sharp knife, cut a diamond pattern about ¼-inch-deep into the baklava, which will make it easier to slice the baklava into pieces later.

6. Transfer to the oven and bake until puffed and golden brown, about 1 hour.

7. Remove from the oven and slowly ladle the cooled syrup over the top, allowing the syrup to sink down into the layers between pours. Let stand at room temperature until all the syrup has been completely absorbed, about 30 minutes and up to overnight. Discard the orange peel.

8. Slice into bars and serve.

MISO CHOCOLATE CAKE

Makes one 9-inch cake

I'm sure it sounds a little weird to see miso in a dessert recipe. If you're familiar at all with the fermented soybean paste, it's likely from Japanese-influenced dishes like soups, dressings, and sauces. But the versatile ingredient is a secret weapon when it comes to desserts, especially those starring chocolate. The umami-rich paste offers a salty-sweet balance to the chocolate's sweetness, bringing balance, depth, and subtle complexity to the final product. Magically, miso makes chocolate taste more chocolatey! If you can't find cans of coconut cream at the market, you can scoop out the cream that rises to the top of an unshaken can of cold full-fat coconut milk. You'll probably need two or three cans' worth.

Coconut Whipped Cream

¾ cup coconut cream (not cream of coconut)
1 tablespoon honey or pure maple syrup
1 teaspoon pure vanilla extract

Cake

Cooking spray
½ cup coconut oil, at room temperature
1 cup sugar
3 tablespoons white miso
2 large eggs
2 teaspoons vanilla extract
2 cups all-purpose flour
¾ cup unsweetened cocoa powder
2 teaspoons baking powder
1½ teaspoons baking soda
1 cup buttermilk
1 cup boiling water
⅓ cup toasted coconut flakes, for serving

1. Make the coconut whipped cream: In a stand mixer fitted with the whisk, combine the coconut cream, honey, and vanilla and beat until light and airy, about 5 minutes. Cover and refrigerate until needed.

2. Make the cake: Preheat the oven to 350°F. Mist a 9-inch cake pan with cooking spray.

3. In a stand mixer fitted with the paddle, combine the coconut oil, sugar, and miso and beat until smooth, about 3 minutes. Add the eggs and vanilla and blend to combine, stopping once or twice to scrape down the sides and bottom of the bowl.

4. In a medium bowl, whisk together the flour, cocoa, baking powder, and baking soda. Add the flour mixture to the mixer and blend until just combined. Add the buttermilk and blend until incorporated. With the mixer on low, carefully add the boiling water and blend until well combined.

5. Pour this mixture into the prepared cake pan. Tap the cake pan on the counter a few times to force out any air bubbles. Give the cake pan a spin to force some batter up the sides, which will provide some lift while baking.

6. Transfer to the oven and bake until a toothpick inserted into the center comes out clean, about 45 minutes. Allow the cake to cool in the pan at least 1 hour before topping.

7. Spread the coconut whipped cream on top of the cake, sprinkle with toasted coconut, slice, and serve.

PAP'S PRETZEL CRUST CHEESE-CAKE SQUARES

Makes 24 squares

In the Symon household, if a cheesecake didn't have a pretzel crust, it was considered an inferior product! New York can keep its pretzel-free crust for all we cared. This was another of Pap's desserts that appeared in heavy rotation at parties and holidays, and you never heard a single complaint from anyone, even the New Yorkers. Cutting the cheesecake into small squares is supposed to keep people from eating too much, but I think it encourages quite the opposite response.

Crust

1½ cups ground pretzels
½ cup graham cracker crumbs
8 tablespoons (1 stick) unsalted butter, melted
¼ cup sugar
Pinch of salt

Filling

3 (8-ounce) packages cream cheese, at room temperature
1 cup sour cream
1 cup sugar
5 large eggs
1 teaspoon pure vanilla extract
1 (8-ounce) jar strawberry preserves

1. Preheat the oven to 300°F.

2. Make the crust: Add the pretzel crumbs to a medium bowl with the graham crackers.

3. Add the melted butter, sugar, and salt and stir to combine. Transfer this mixture into a 9 × 13-inch glass baking dish and use a 1-cup measuring cup to evenly press the mixture onto the bottom of the pan.

4. Make the filling: In a stand mixer fitted with the paddle, beat the cream cheese on medium speed until softened, stopping to scrape down the sides and bottom of the bowl a few times. Add the sour cream and beat until combined. Add the sugar and beat until combined. With the mixer on low, add the eggs one at a time, allowing them to become fully incorporated before adding the next. Add the vanilla and beat until combined.

5. Pour the filling into the baking dish and bake until the filling is set, about 1 hour. Let the cheesecake cool while you make the topping.

6. In a small saucepan, melt the strawberry preserves over low heat until smooth. (If you prefer a seedless topping, strain through a fine-mesh sieve.) Pour the strawberry sauce onto the cheesecake and smooth with a spatula to an even layer.

7. Let the cheesecake cool at room temperature for 30 minutes to 1 hour before slicing into 24 squares (the cheesecake is easier to slice when warm). Refrigerate until completely chilled before serving.

CHOCOLATE PUMPKIN PIE

If a flourless chocolate cake and a classic pumpkin pie had a love child, it would be this silky, sinful dessert. I made a version of it for Thanksgiving during the second season of *The Chew* and it absolutely blew up on my social media pages. You can cheat a little by using a store-bought crust.

Makes one 9-inch pie

Pie Crust

1¼ cups all-purpose flour, plus more for rolling
8 tablespoons (1 stick) cold unsalted butter, cut into small cubes
½ teaspoon kosher salt
½ teaspoon granulated sugar
2 to 4 tablespoons ice-cold water

Filling

6 ounces semisweet chocolate, chopped
3 ounces bittersweet chocolate, chopped
4 tablespoons (½ stick) cold unsalted butter, cut into small cubes
1 (15-ounce) can pure pumpkin
1 (12-ounce) can evaporated milk
¾ cup packed light brown sugar
3 large eggs
1 tablespoon cornstarch
1 teaspoon pure vanilla extract
¾ teaspoon ground cinnamon
¾ teaspoon ground ginger
½ teaspoon kosher salt
¼ teaspoon freshly grated nutmeg
Pinch of ground cloves

1. Make the pie crust: In a food processor, combine the flour, butter, salt, and granulated sugar and pulse until the mixture resembles coarse sand with small marbles of butter remaining. Sprinkle in 2 tablespoons of ice water and pulse until crumbly and the dough holds together when squeezed. If the dough appears too dry, sprinkle in another tablespoon or two of cold water, being careful to not overmix the dough. Transfer the dough to a plastic bag, press into the shape of a disc, and refrigerate for 1 hour.

2. Preheat the oven to 425°F.

3. On a lightly floured surface, roll the dough out to a 12-inch round. Carefully press the dough into a 9-inch pie pan. Trim the dough to leave a 1-inch overhang all around. Flute or fold under the excess dough. Fit a large piece of parchment paper into the pie shell and fill with pie weights or dried beans.

4. Transfer to the oven and bake until golden brown, about 15 minutes. Leave the oven on but reduce the temperature to 325°F.

5. Make the filling: In the top of a double boiler set over medium-low heat, combine the semisweet chocolate, bittersweet chocolate, and butter. Cook, stirring frequently, until melted and smooth. Remove from the heat.

6. In a large bowl, combine the pumpkin, evaporated milk, brown sugar, eggs, cornstarch, vanilla, cinnamon, ginger, salt, nutmeg, and cloves and stir to combine. Fold in the melted chocolate.

7. Place the pie pan on a baking sheet, pour the filling into the pie crust, and bake until the filling is set, about 1 hour. Refrigerate until cooled completely before serving.

BANANA ESPRESSO PUDDING

Serves 6

I absolutely love banana pudding, and this dish is like a grown-up version of it thanks to the coffee pastry cream and the cinnamon/vanilla-infused whipped cream. You certainly don't need to be a pastry whiz to pull it off. When it comes to serving, you can go with one large trifle bowl, individual parfait glasses, or even small mason jars tucked into ice for serve-yourself backyard barbecues. It's the kind of dessert that is totally appropriate in the summer after a platter of ribs, or after a hearty braised-meat dinner in the dead of winter.

Coffee Pastry Cream

2 cups whole milk
½ cup granulated sugar
Pinch of salt
2 tablespoons instant espresso powder
1 large egg
4 large egg yolks
¼ cup cornstarch
⅓ cup mascarpone cheese
2 tablespoons cold butter
1 teaspoon pure vanilla extract

Cinnamon Whipped Cream

1 cup heavy cream
2 tablespoons powdered sugar
½ teaspoon pure vanilla extract
Pinch of ground cinnamon

Assembly

2 cups Nilla wafers
4 bananas, sliced

1. Make the coffee pastry cream: In a medium saucepan, combine the milk, ¼ cup of the granulated sugar, and the salt and bring to a simmer over medium-high heat. Whisk in the espresso powder and reduce the heat to low.

2. In a large bowl, whisk together the whole egg, egg yolks, cornstarch, and remaining ¼ cup granulated sugar and whisk until smooth. Whisking constantly, slowly add half of the hot milk mixture to the egg mixture. Pour this warmed egg mixture into the saucepan with remaining milk and whisk to combine.

3. Return the saucepan to low heat and stir with a silicone spatula, scraping the bottom and sides of the pot, until thickened and small bubbles form on the surface. Remove from the heat, add the mascarpone, butter, and vanilla and stir to combine. Transfer to a bowl and cover with plastic wrap, pushing the plastic onto the surface of the mixture to prevent a film from forming. Refrigerate until needed, up to 1 day ahead.

4. Make the cinnamon whipped cream: In a large bowl, combine the cream, powdered sugar, vanilla, and cinnamon and whisk until medium-stiff peaks form.

5. To assemble, place a layer of the coffee pastry cream in the bottom of 6 parfait glasses, followed by Nilla wafers and sliced bananas. Repeat this process. Top with the cinnamon whipped cream and refrigerate for 1 hour or up to overnight.

NO-BAKE BLUEBERRY LEMON PIE

This ideal summertime pie was truly a labor of love—my love, Katie's labor! LOL. It's fresh and creamy and bursting with ripe fruit flavor. You don't even have to turn on the oven, but you do have to let the pie refrigerate overnight.

Makes one 9-inch pie

Blueberry Puree

1 cup blueberries
2 tablespoons sugar
Juice of ½ lemon
Pinch of salt

Crust

2½ cups graham cracker crumbs
1½ sticks (6 ounces) unsalted butter, melted
¼ cup sugar
Pinch of salt

Filling

2 cups heavy cream
½ cup whole milk
1 (¼-ounce) envelope unflavored gelatin powder
1 (16-ounce) package cream cheese, at room temperature
⅔ cup sugar
Grated zest and juice of 2 lemons
Lemon zest, for garnish
Blueberries, for garnish

1. Make the blueberry puree: In a saucepan, combine the blueberries, sugar, lemon juice, and salt and bring to a boil over medium-high heat. Reduce the heat to maintain a simmer and cook, stirring, until the sugar dissolves and the blueberries begin to burst, about 2 minutes. Carefully transfer to a blender or food processer and puree until smooth. Cover and refrigerate until needed.

2. Add the graham cracker crumbs to a medium bowl and stir in the melted butter, sugar, and salt to combine. Scrape this mixture into a 9-inch springform pan and use a 1-cup measuring cup to evenly press the mixture onto the bottom and one-third of the way up the sides of the pan.

3. Make the filling: In a stand mixer fitted with the whisk, beat the cream until medium stiff peaks are formed, about 3 minutes. Transfer to a bowl and set aside. Clean the mixer bowl.

4. In a small saucepan, whisk together the milk and gelatin and set aside for 5 minutes. Set the pan over medium heat and cook, stirring occasionally, until the gelatin melts. Remove from the heat and set aside to cool before adding to the cream cheese.

5. In a stand mixer fitted with the paddle attachment, beat the cream cheese and sugar until smooth. Add the milk-gelatin mixture, lemon zest, and lemon juice and blend until smooth, stopping once or twice to scrape down the sides and bottom of the bowl. Add half of the whipped cream and blend until smooth. Fold the rest of the whipped cream in by hand.

6. Pour the filling into the pie crust and smooth the surface with a spatula. Use a spoon to drizzle thin lines of blueberry puree across the surface. Drag a toothpick across the lines to create a swirled pattern (you can also just add the blueberry puree to the top and skip swirling for more of a layered look). Refrigerate overnight.

7. Carefully remove the sides of the pan, slice into 8 wedges, and serve.

LEMON COCONUT CAKE ROLL

Serves 6

Coconut cake is my all-time favorite dessert. For as long as I can remember, every single one of my birthday cakes has been a coconut cake. When I was a kid, it was the famous lemon coconut cake from Cleveland's Hough Bakery: a simple white cake with lemon filling and coconut frosting. Lizzie's mom, Sherla, makes a great one, as does my longtime restaurant pastry chef Summer Genetti. Katie and I played around with a million different versions trying to land on something that is light, lemony, and loaded with coconut flavor, but without that superrich buttercream. We ended up doing this as a roll because it just worked out the best (and is truly so simple to make). If you like coconut cake as I do, give this recipe a whirl. I promise it will be your go-to from here on out. It's never been easier to find great-quality packaged lemon curd at the store, which makes this cake even simpler to put together. When shopping for coconut cream, make sure that you don't grab cream of coconut by mistake. They are different products.

Cake

Cooking spray
1 cup all-purpose flour
1½ cups granulated sugar
1 teaspoon baking powder
¾ teaspoon baking soda
½ teaspoon kosher salt
4 large eggs, separated and at room temperature
½ cup vegetable oil
½ cup full-fat coconut milk
2 teaspoons coconut extract
Grated zest of 2 lemons
2 large egg whites, at room temperature
Pinch of cream of tartar
2 tablespoons powdered sugar

Filling

1 cup heavy cream
½ cup mascarpone cheese
¼ cup coconut cream (not cream of coconut)
1 teaspoon coconut extract
1 tablespoon powdered sugar

Assembly

½ cup lemon curd
1 cup sweetened shredded coconut
1 tablespoon powdered sugar
Grated zest of 1 lemon

1. Make the cake: Preheat the oven to 350°F. Line a half-sheet pan with parchment paper. Mist the paper and sides of the pan evenly with cooking spray.

2. In a medium bowl, whisk together the flour, 1 cup of the granulated sugar, the baking powder, baking soda, and salt. In a large bowl, whisk together the 4 egg yolks, vegetable oil, coconut milk, and coconut extract. Add half of the flour mixture to the wet ingredients and whisk to combine. Add the remaining flour mixture and the lemon zest and whisk to combine.

(recipe continues)

3. In a stand mixer fitted with the whisk, combine the 6 egg whites and the cream of tartar. Blend on medium speed until foamy, about 1 minute. With the machine running, slowly add the remaining ½ cup granulated sugar. Continue blending until the whites form stiff, shiny peaks, about 3 minutes.

4. Add ⅓ cup of the egg whites to the cake batter and whisk until smooth. Use a rubber spatula to gently fold the remaining egg whites into the cake batter, being careful not to deflate. Pour the batter onto the prepared sheet pan and smooth it out to an even layer.

5. Transfer to the oven and bake until golden brown and the cake springs back when pressed in the center, about 25 minutes.

6. Dust a large piece of parchment paper with the powdered sugar. When the cake is cool enough to handle, carefully loosen the parchment paper from the sheet pan and invert the cake onto the sugar-dusted parchment paper. Carefully remove the top piece of parchment paper. Working from a long side, roll the cake into a tight roll. Place it seam-side down on a sheet pan, cover, and refrigerate for at least 1 hour or up to 5 days.

7. Make the filling: In a stand mixer fitted with the whisk, combine the dairy cream, mascarpone, coconut cream, coconut extract, and powdered sugar and blend on medium speed until the cream holds stiff peaks, about 3 minutes. Refrigerate if not using right away (but use within 2 days).

8. Assemble the cake: Remove the cake from the refrigerator and carefully unroll it toward you. Use a spatula to evenly spread the lemon curd across the entire surface of the cake, spreading it all the way to the edges. Spread the filling evenly on top of the lemon curd, taking it all the way to the edges but leaving a 1-inch border on the far end. Evenly sprinkle the shredded coconut across the entire surface and gently press it into the filling. Working from the long end closest to you, roll the cake into a tight roll and place it seam-side down on a platter. Dust the top with the powdered sugar and garnish with the lemon zest.

9. Slice into six 2-inch-thick slices and serve. The rolled cake will hold up to 5 days in the fridge, but wait to dust with the powdered sugar and lemon zest until just before serving.

STRAWBERRY PIE WITH BROWN-BUTTER CRUST

Lightly browning butter is such a simple way to add incredible depth of flavor to everything from whipped potatoes (page 250) to grilled fish. But where it really shines is in desserts, as it brings a measure of nutty sweetness to everything from crusts to fillings. Make this heavenly pie in early summer when strawberries are bright, plump, and fragrant. If it's not strawberry season, use whatever ripe, juicy berries you can find at the market.

Pie Crust

- 1½ sticks (6 ounces) unsalted butter
- 1¾ cups all-purpose flour, plus more for rolling
- 2 tablespoons granulated sugar
- ¼ teaspoon salt
- 1½ teaspoons distilled white or cider vinegar
- 3 tablespoons ice-cold water, plus more if needed

Filling

- 6 cups sliced strawberries
- Grated zest and juice of 1 small lemon
- 3 (¼-ounce) envelopes unflavored gelatin powder
- ¾ cup granulated sugar
- Pinch of salt
- 1 teaspoon pure vanilla extract

Topping

- 1½ cups heavy cream
- 2 tablespoons powdered sugar
- 1 teaspoon almond extract (optional)

1. Make the pie crust: In a saucepan, melt the butter over medium heat and cook, stirring frequently, until the butter begins to brown and smell nutty, about 5 minutes. Transfer to an 8 × 8-inch pan and refrigerate until the butter is firm. Cut the butter into small cubes and keep very cold.

2. In a food processor, combine the flour, granulated sugar, and salt and pulse to combine. Add one-third of the diced cold butter and process until completely combined. Add the remaining two-thirds of butter and pulse until the mixture resembles coarse sand with small marbles of butter remaining. Add the vinegar and pulse to blend. While pulsing, gradually add the ice water until the dough just comes together in the bowl. Add more ice water, 1 tablespoon at a time, if needed.

3. Turn the dough out onto a clean surface and knead it into a cohesive ball. Wrap with plastic, press it into the shape of a disc, and refrigerate for at least 1 hour.

(recipe continues)

4. On a lightly floured surface, roll the dough out to a round slightly larger than a 9-inch pie pan. Carefully press the dough into a pie pan. Trim the dough to leave a 1-inch overhang all around. Flute or fold under the excess dough. Refrigerate the pie shell until very cold, about 20 minutes.

5. Preheat the oven to 375°F.

6. Fit a large piece of parchment paper into the pie shell and fill with pie weights or dried beans. Bake for 25 minutes. Remove the parchment paper and pie weights or dried beans and bake until golden brown, about 20 minutes. Allow to cool before filling.

7. Make the filling: In a medium bowl, combine 4 cups of the strawberries and the lemon zest.

8. In a small bowl, combine ½ cup water and the gelatin. Let stand until fully bloomed and hydrated, about 5 minutes.

9. In a blender or food processor, combine the remaining 2 cups strawberries, the lemon juice, granulated sugar, salt, vanilla, and ¼ cup water and process until smooth. Transfer to a medium saucepan over medium heat. When the mixture comes to a strong simmer, add the gelatin mixture and whisk until smooth. Remove from the heat and allow to cool before adding the mixture to the strawberry/lemon zest mixture. Stir to combine.

10. Pour the strawberry mixture into the pie crust and smooth out the top. Refrigerate until very cold and set.

11. Make the topping: In a stand mixer fitted with the whisk, combine the cream, powdered sugar, and almond extract (if using) and beat until stiff peaks are formed. Spread the whipped cream evenly across the entire pie and refrigerate until serving.

Batch Cocktails

One of the best party hacks that we've added to our entertaining repertoire is the batch cocktail. Instead of whipping up individual drinks for guests as they arrive, we make a big batch of one of our favorite cocktails ahead of time. This way, when guests do appear, all you need to do is pour, garnish, and serve! This brilliant system allows you to spend more time welcoming guests and less time fumbling with spirits, mixers, barware, and glassware. All you need is a large pitcher and the recipes that follow.

When making batch cocktails, it's important to use good-quality spirits, measure the ingredients, and always go with fresh-squeezed citrus whenever possible. To keep the drinks from getting too watery, don't add ice to the whole batch, but rather to the individual glasses as they are poured. Another trick I love is to make fruit-flavored ice cubes ahead of time. That way, as they melt, they properly dilute the alcohol while infusing even more flavor into the drink.

Remember, the first 15 minutes of a party often sets the tone for the entire night. Why not kick it off the right way with a tasty (and speedy) concoction?

VODKA PUNCH

Serves 8

This simple but delicious cocktail is always a crowd-pleaser. It's pretty fruit-forward, so it won't land people under the table. When making ice cubes ahead of time, I like adding berries or small pieces of seasonal fruit to the tray cells. It's a small touch that makes a big impression.

Lemon/Lime Ice Cubes

Fresh blueberries or blackberries
Fresh strawberries, hulled and quartered
1 quart lemonade or limeade

Punch

2 cups vodka
¾ cup orange liqueur, such as Grand Mariner or Cointreau
1½ cups cranberry juice
1½ cups pineapple juice
2¼ cups ginger ale
Seltzer, for serving
Orange slices, for garnish

1. Make the lemon/lime ice cubes: The night before, sprinkle a few berries and strawberry quarters into each ice cube tray slot, top with lemonade or limeade, and freeze. When frozen, pop the cubes out of the tray and store in a zip-top bag and return to the freezer.

2. Make the punch: In a large pitcher or punch bowl, combine the vodka, orange liqueur, cranberry juice, and pineapple juice and stir to blend. Top with the ginger ale and stir.

3. Fill highball glasses with the lemon/lime ice cubes, add the punch, top with seltzer, and garnish with orange slices.

KENTUCKY MULE

Serves 8

This popular spin on the Moscow Mule swaps bourbon for the customary vodka, giving the cocktail a spicier and mature flavor profile. In my opinion, the better quality ginger beer you use, the better this drink becomes. If you happen to have those snazzy copper mugs, by all means bust them out!

2 cups bourbon
¾ cup fresh lime juice
  (about 6 limes)
5¼ cups ginger beer or ginger ale

Ice cubes
Seltzer, for serving
Lime wedges, for garnish
Fresh mint, for garnish

In a half-gallon pitcher, combine the bourbon, lime juice, and ginger beer and stir to blend. Pour into ice-filled glasses and top with a splash of seltzer. Garnish with a lime wedge and mint sprig.

CAMPARI SPRITZ

Serves 8

The Campari Spritz is my go-to cocktail when I'm kicking off a night on the town. It's not too boozy and the slightly bitter notes of the Campari do wonders to stimulate your appetite. If you like Aperol Spritzes but find them a touch too sweet, you will probably love this version.

3 cups prosecco
3 cups Campari
1¾ cups seltzer

Ice cubes
Large green olives, for garnish

In a half-gallon pitcher, combine the prosecco, Campari, and seltzer and gently stir to blend. Pour into ice-filled highball glasses and garnish with 1 or 2 olives per glass.

LIMEADE RUM COCKTAIL

Serves 8

This is a simple riff on the brilliant Mojito, a classic summer sipper if ever there was one. If I'm chilling poolside or grilling up a storm, chances are good I'm knocking back a few of these fizzy tropical cocktails.

6 cups limeade (see Note)
2 cups light rum
Ice cubes
Seltzer, for serving

Lime wedges or wheels, for squeezing
Mint sprigs, for garnish

In a half-gallon pitcher, combine the limeade and rum and gently stir to blend. Pour into ice-filled Collins glasses and top with a splash of seltzer. Finish with a squeeze of lime and garnish with a mint sprig.

Symon Says

If you have extra limeade, freeze into cubes the night before to use in the cocktails.

FROZEN OLD FASHIONED

Serves 8

This recipe is pure genius if I don't mind saying so! I love Old Fashioneds in fall and winter but sometimes find them out of place in the summertime. The solution: Old Fashioned slushies! This version balances the sweetness of bourbon and simple syrup with the zippy fruitiness of tart cherries. Wait until the first guests arrive to crank up the blender!

2 cups tart cherry juice
½ cup turbinado sugar, such as
   Sugar In The Raw
2 cups bourbon

16 dashes Angostura bitters
4 cups ice
Thick orange twists, for garnish

1. The night before, fill two ice cube trays with tart cherry juice. When frozen, pop the cubes out of the tray and store in a zip-top bag in the freezer.

2. In a small saucepan, combine ½ cup water and the sugar and bring to a simmer over medium-high heat. Whisk until the sugar is dissolved, then store the simple syrup in the fridge to thoroughly chill before using.

3. In a high-powered blender, combine the bourbon, bitters, ¼ cup of the simple syrup, the tart cherry ice cubes, and plain ice cubes and blend until smooth.

4. Pour into rocks glasses and garnish with orange twists.

MULLED WINE

Serves 8

Mulled wine might be one of the original batch cocktails! Dating back literally centuries, the technique of flavoring wine with spices was used by the ancient Greeks and copied by others ever since. Start with a good-quality dry red wine and you really can't go wrong. And if you happen to have a bottle of Cognac on hand, a wee splash on top really sends it to another level! A mug of this warms my soul more than a fire in the hearth.

2 (750 ml) bottles dry red wine
2 cups apple cider
6 tablespoons honey
6 chai-spiced tea bags

1-inch-wide strip of orange zest
8 cinnamon sticks, for garnish
Cognac, for serving (optional)

1. In a large saucepan, combine the wine, cider, and honey and bring to a simmer over medium heat, stirring until the honey has dissolved. Reduce the heat to maintain a gentle simmer, add the tea bags and orange zest, and simmer for 15 minutes. Discard the tea bags and orange zest, cover, and keep warm until serving.

2. Ladle the hot mulled wine into mugs or heat-safe glasses, garnish each with a cinnamon stick, and top with a shot of Cognac (if using).

APEROL AND CITRUS SLUSHIES

Serves 8

The only beverage more refreshing than an Aperol Spritz is an Aperol Slushie! I might install a slushie machine in my kitchen to provide a never-ending summer supply! This blend of fresh-squeezed citrus and sweet-tart lemonade and limeade melds perfectly with the slightly bitter Italian liqueur.

1 cup lemonade
1 cup limeade
1 cup freshly squeezed orange juice (about 3 oranges)
1 cup freshly squeezed grapefruit juice (about 3 grapefruits)
Ice cubes
3 cups Aperol

1. To make the lemon-lime ice cubes, the night before, in a large pitcher, combine the lemonade and limeade and stir to blend. Pour into two ice cube trays to freeze into lemon-lime ice cubes.

2. To make the orange-grapefruit ice cubes, the night before, in a large pitcher, combine the orange juice and grapefruit juice and stir to blend. Pour into two ice cube trays to freeze into cubes.

3. When frozen, pop the cubes out of each tray and store in separate zip-top bags in the freezer for up to 1 week.

4. In a high-powered blender, combine equal amounts of lemon-lime ice cubes, orange-grapefruit ice cubes, and regular ice cubes with the Aperol and process until smooth.

5. Serve in tall glasses or insulated tumblers.

COLD BREW MARTINI

Serves 8

The Espresso Martini made a huge comeback recently, but it never went out of style at my house. I'm not ashamed to admit that we love the coffee-flavored cocktail and its pick-me-up qualities. This version swaps the espresso for cold-brew coffee and the vodka for bourbon, which I feel melds better with the coffee and Kahlúa. This is such a festive holiday sipper.

3½ cups cold-brew coffee
1¾ cups bourbon
1¾ cups sweetened vanilla oat milk

1 cup Kahlúa
Ice cubes

1. In a half-gallon pitcher, combine the coffee, bourbon, oat milk, and Kahlúa and stir to blend. Refrigerate until cold.

2. Fill a 1-pint mason jar or cocktail shaker about three-quarters full with the cocktail mixture, cover, and shake vigorously until frothy. If using a mason jar, add ice and serve. If using a cocktail shaker, pour into a tall ice-filled glass. Repeat for as many people as you're serving.

SUMMER RUM FIZZ

Serves 8

This is another twist on sweet, citrusy Mojitos. For me, rum, mint, and lime cocktails always stir up memories of carefree beach vacations. Who doesn't love sipping pineapple-garnished bevvies while doing nothing but staring at the shimmering water. Make these in summer when your garden is swimming in fresh mint.

2 cups loosely packed fresh mint leaves
½ cup sugar
3¾ cups light rum
2 cups fresh lime juice (about 16 limes)

2 cups Cointreau
Ice cubes
Seltzer, for serving
Mint sprigs, for garnish
Pineapple wedges, for garnish

In a half-gallon pitcher, combine the mint leaves and sugar and muddle using a muddler until the mint begins to break down and the sugar dissolves. Add the rum, lime juice, and Cointreau and stir to blend. Pour into ice-filled highball glasses, top with seltzer, and garnish with mint sprigs and pineapple wedges.

PIMM'S CUP

Serves 8

You don't have to be watching a match at Wimbledon to sip on this quintessentially British beverage. This refreshing, low-alcohol cocktail has such a unique and delicious flavor profile. The next time you find yourself at the liquor store, pick up a bottle of Pimm's and taste for yourself.

3 cups Pimm's No. 1 Cup
4½ cups lemon seltzer
1 cup fresh lemon juice
   (about 4 lemons)
12 thin cucumber slices

12 thin lemon slices
12 strawberries, hulled and halved
Crushed ice (see Note)
Seltzer, for serving
Fresh basil sprigs, for garnish

In a half-gallon pitcher, combine the Pimm's, lemon seltzer, and lemon juice and stir to blend. Add the cucumber slices, lemon slices, and strawberries to the pitcher and stir. Fill highball glasses with crushed ice, pour in the cocktail, and add a few pieces of fruit and cucumbers to each glass. Top with seltzer and garnish with a sprig of basil.

> **Symon Says**
>
> To make crushed ice, place ice cubes in a high-powered blender such as a Vitamix and blend on high until the ice is coarsely broken down. Alternatively, you can place the ice in a large zip-top bag and crush it with the back of a skillet.

SYMON SIPPER

Serves 8

This drink has been on the menu at Mabel's BBQ since Day One and it has always been one of the top sellers. Picture yourself sitting outside on a sweltering August day when someone hands you a tall, frost-covered glass filled with sweet tea, lemon, and a little nip of whiskey. Now we're talking! This version absolutely rocks.

⅔ cup turbinado sugar, such as Sugar In The Raw
8 tea bags (black tea)
1 cup fresh lemon juice (about 6 lemons)

1 cup bourbon
Crushed ice (see Note) or ice cubes
8 (1-inch-wide) lemon twists, for serving

1. In a small saucepan, combine ⅔ cup water and the sugar and bring to a simmer over medium-high heat. Whisk until the sugar is fully dissolved, transfer the simple syrup to a heatproof container, then store in the fridge until chilled.

2. In a medium saucepan, bring 5 cups water to a boil over high heat. Add the tea bags, cover, remove from the heat, and steep for 5 minutes. Remove and discard the tea bags. Refrigerate until chilled.

3. In a half-gallon pitcher, combine the chilled tea, 1 cup of the simple syrup, lemon juice, bourbon, and 2 cups water and stir to blend. Refrigerate until serving.

4. Fill highball glasses with crushed ice, pour in the cocktail, and garnish each with a lemon twist.

Symon Says

To make crushed ice, place ice cubes in a high-powered blender such as a Vitamix and blend on high until the ice is coarsely broken down.

BOURBON CRUSH

Serves 8

This tasty twist on a Bourbon Smash will appeal even to guests who think they don't like whiskey. The muddled blueberries and basil tame the bourbon's heat while providing a summery boost. Combined with plenty of fresh lemon juice and garnished with more fruit and herbs, this is the perfect batch cocktail for a casual garden party.

1⅓ cups turbinado sugar, such as
    Sugar In The Raw
2 cups blueberries
20 fresh basil leaves
4 cups bourbon

2 cups fresh lemon juice (about
    10 lemons)
Ice cubes
Angostura bitters, for serving
Fresh basil sprigs and
    blueberries, for garnish

1. In a small saucepan, combine 1⅓ cups water and the sugar and bring to a simmer over medium-high heat. Whisk until the sugar is dissolved. Transfer the simple syrup to a heatproof container and store in the fridge until ready to use.

2. In a half-gallon pitcher, combine the blueberries and basil leaves and muddle with a muddler until they begin to break down. Add the bourbon, lemon juice, and 2 cups of the simple syrup and stir to combine. Strain through a fine-mesh sieve and discard the solids. Return the mixture to the pitcher and keep refrigerated until needed.

3. Pour into ice-filled highball glasses, add a few dashes of bitters, and garnish with a sprig of basil and a blueberry.

A *Fix It with Food* Index for Recipes in *Simply Symon Suppers*

RECIPE	PAGE	FLOUR-FREE	DAIRY-FREE	MEAT-FREE
Grandma Pie with Mozz and Basil	53			X
+ Antipasto Salad	54	X		
Gnocchi with Brown Butter, Peas, and Mushrooms	58			X
+ Grilled Asparagus and Lemon	61			X
Grilled Lamb Chops	62	X	X	
+ Mint Sauce	64	X	X	X
+ Lemon Potatoes	64	X	X	X
+ Horta	65	X	X	X
Manicotti Stuffed with Ricotta and Spinach	68			X
+ Snap Pea Salad	70	X		
Braised Beef Stew	73		X	
+ Smashed Peas	74	X		X
+ Grilled Red Onion Salad	74	X		X
Roasted Salmon	77	X	X	
+ Shaved Cucumbers and Radishes	78	X	X	X
+ Creamy Dill Sauce	78	X		X

RECIPE	PAGE	FLOUR-FREE	DAIRY-FREE	MEAT-FREE
Whole Grilled Snapper	85	X	X	
+ Grill-Roasted Tomatoes	86	X	X	X
+ Anchovy Bread	86		X	
Sticky Pork Ribs	89	X	X	
+ Coconut Rice	90	X	X	X
+ Papaya Relish	90	X	X	X
Swordfish Kebabs	92	X		
+ Radish Cucumber Salad	94	X	X	X
+ Lemon Yogurt Sauce	94	X		X
Grilled Skirt Steak with Romesco Sauce	95	X	X	
+ Toasted Bread Salad	97		X	X
Smoked Pulled Pork	98	X	X	
+ Liz's Biscuits	101			X
+ Cabbage and Carrot Slaw	102	X	X	X
Grilled Scallops	104	X	X	
+ Charred Cauliflower Steaks	106	X	X	X
+ Gremolata	107	X	X	X

RECIPE	PAGE	FLOUR-FREE	DAIRY-FREE	MEAT-FREE
Grilled Lobster with Lime-Jalapeño Butter	109	X		
+ Spicy Old Bay Corn on the Cob	110	X	X	X
Grilled Flank Steak	113	X	X	X
+ Fire-Roasted Potatoes	114	X		
+ Bacon-Onion Jam	114	X	X	
Grilled Salmon Steaks	117	X	X	
+ Grilled Bok Choy	118	X	X	X
+ Mustard Sauce	118	X		X
Grilled Chicken Paillard	122	X	X	
+ Charred Broccoli Rabe with Grilled Lemons	123	X	X	X
Crunchy Fried Chicken	125		X	
+ Throwdown Fried Chicken Sauce	127	X		X
+ Jojo Fries	127			X
Shrimp Scampi with Linguine	129			
+ Green Beans and Radicchio	130	X	X	X

RECIPE	PAGE	FLOUR-FREE	DAIRY-FREE	MEAT-FREE
Pork Roast with Cider-Braised Root Vegetables and Pan Gravy	137		X	
Marsala and Mushroom Pasta Bake	138			X
+ Shaved Brussels Sprout Salad	141	X		X
Stovetop Mac and Cheese	142			X
+ Bitter Greens Salad	145	X	X	
Sweet Potato Pierogies	146			X
+ Roasted Kielbasa with Pickled Mustard Seeds	149	X	X	
Chicken and Prosciutto Rolls	150	X		
+ Roasted Acorn Squash	153	X	X	X
+ Spinach Salad	153	X		X
Turkey and Sweet Potato Pie	154			
+ Roasted Radicchio Salad with Pecans	157	X	X	X
Maple-Glazed Roast Chicken	159	X	X	
+ Butternut Squash Puree	160	X		X
+ Endive and Apple Salad	160	X	X	X

RECIPE	PAGE	FLOUR-FREE	DAIRY-FREE	MEAT-FREE
Cast-Iron Rib Eyes	163	X		
+ Crispy Smashed Potatoes	164	X	X	X
+ Frisée and Bacon Salad	165	X	X	
Shells with Clams	167		X	
+ Classic Caesar Salad	169			
Braciole	172	X		
+ Parmesan Polenta	174	X		X
+ Pomodoro Sauce	174	X		X
Seafood Stew	177	X	X	
+ Saffron Aioli	178	X	X	X
+ Grilled Bread	178		X	X
Pan-Roasted Duck with Orange Sauce and Parsley Salad	181	X		
Baked Ziti	185			X
+ Escarole with Anchovy-Garlic Bread Crumbs	186		X	

RECIPE	PAGE	FLOUR-FREE	DAIRY-FREE	MEAT-FREE
Sunday Sauce	193			
+ Ricotta Cavatelli	194			X
+ Mom's Salad	194	X		X
Cast-Iron Smash Burgers	199			
+ Double-Cooked French Fries	200	X	X	X
+ Extra-Crispy Onion Rings	200			X
Pork Tenderloin Schnitzel	203		X	
+ Mushroom Gravy	204			
+ Cauliflower Puree	204	X		X
+ Crispy Leeks	205		X	X
Chicken Paprikash	207			
+ Spaetzle	208			X
American Goulash	211			
Classic Meatloaf	212		X	
+ Root Vegetable Puree	215	X		X
+ Celery Salad	215	X	X	X
Pork Meatballs in Sauerkraut	217		X	
+ Apple and Brussels Sprouts Salad	218	X	X	X

RECIPE	PAGE	FLOUR-FREE	DAIRY-FREE	MEAT-FREE
+ Apple-Pear Sauce	218	X	X	X
Stuffed Cabbage in Tomato Sauce	221		X	
Beef Stew	225		X	
+ Popovers	226			
+ Shaved Carrot Salad	226	X	X	X
Chicken Pot Pie	227			
+ Shaved Mushroom Salad	230	X	X	X
Potato and Sweet Potato Pancakes	233		X	X
+ Poached Eggs	234	X	X	X
+ Pear and Crispy-Quinoa Salad	235	X		X
French Onion Soup	237			
+ Wheat Berry, Roasted Squash, and Shaved Brussels Sprouts Salad	238			X
Pierogi "Lasagna" Casserole	241			
+ Kohlrabi and Green Apple Salad	243	X	X	X

RECIPE	PAGE	FLOUR-FREE	DAIRY-FREE	MEAT-FREE
Pastrami-Smoked Prime Rib	249	X	X	
+ Brown Butter Whipped Potatoes	250	X		X
+ Charred Brussels Sprouts	253	X	X	X
+ Horseradish Sauce	253	X		X
Corned Beef and Cabbage	254		X	
+ Irish Soda Bread	257			X
Smoked Ham with Bourbon Glaze	258	X		
+ Hash Browns and Cheddar Casserole	261	X		X
+ Green Bean Casserole	262			X
Mom's Other Lasagna	265			
+ Mozzarella-Stuffed Garlic Bread	269			X
Classic Symon Turkey	270	X		
+ Pap's Corn Pudding	273			X
+ Turkey Gravy	273			
+ Classic Dressing	275			

Holidays

Acknowledgments

I wouldn't be where I am today without the love, trust, and support of my wife, Liz, who is so understanding about the demands of work and travel. The same goes for Mom, Dad, and my grandparents, who inspired in me not only a love for food, but a love of people, regardless of background. Thanks also to Kyle, Krista, Emmy, and Butchie. Being able to be so close to them on a daily basis not only inspires me but fills my life with meaning and joy that I didn't know I could have.

Boundless thanks and appreciation are due to culinary director, Katie Pickens, whose painstaking recipe testing guarantees that every dish in this book will come out great. While working side by side for more than a decade, Katie has become not only a valued member of the team, but a cherished member of the Symon family.

Thanks to my manager of nearly twenty years, Scott Feldman of Two-Twelve Management, a real mensch who represents me as though I'm his only client. Nobody understands the food and media arena better than he does. Credit goes to Margaret Riley King with William Morris Agency, a team that always manages to ink the perfect deal.

Thank you to my Food Network family for allowing me to teach, inspire, and entertain home cooks for the better part of twenty years.

This is the seventh book that I've collaborated on with Douglas Trattner, who not only is my coauthor, but also a patient friend who keeps these projects rolling along despite my challenging schedule.

Brilliant photographer Ed Anderson, along with Maeve Sheridan, have a knack for capturing the true spirit of a book while making every dish look as delicious on the page as it does on the plate. It is always a privilege to collaborate with Ed and his team. I also had the pleasure and honor to once again collaborate with super-stylist Susan Spungen, who has the magic touch when it comes to styling. Our books are always better when she is involved.

And, of course, Raquel Pelzel, our meticulous editor, dependable guide, and constant cheerleader at Clarkson. Over the course of four cookbooks, it has been her attention to detail that has resulted in such successful finished products.

Index

Note: Page references in *italics* indicate photographs.

Michael Symon is a James Beard Award–winning chef and restaurateur, an Emmy-winning television personality, and a bestselling author. He is the host of *Symon's Dinners Cooking Out* and *BBQ USA*, cohost of *BBQ Brawl*, and former cohost of ABC's *The Chew*, and has the Symon Home line of appliances and home goods on HSN. This is his eighth cookbook.

Clarkson Potter/Publishers
New York
clarksonpotter.com

Cover design: Robert Diaz
Cover photographs: Ed Anderson